Manager's Guide to Business Planning

Other titles in the Briefcase Books series include:

To learn more about titles in the Briefcase Books series go to
www.briefcasebooks.com

Manager's Guide to Business Planning

Peter J. Capezio

New York Chicago San Francisco Lisbon
London Madrid Mexico City Milan New Delhi
San Juan Seoul Singapore Sydney Toronto

1 2 3 4 5 6 7 8 9 0 DOC/DOC 0 1 0 9

ISBN 978-0-07-162800-6
MHID   0-07-162800-2

This is a CWL Publishing Enterprises book developed for McGraw-Hill by CWL Publishing Enterprises, Inc., Madison, Wisconsin, www.cwlpub.com.

McGraw-Hill books are available at special quantity discounts to use as premiums and sales promotions, or for use in corporate training programs. To contact a representative please e-mail us at bulksales@mcgraw-hill.com.

Contents

Preface

I wrote the *Manager's Guide to Business Planning* to provide business-people with a complete perspective on the planning process. A main premise in this book is that planning and execution go hand in hand. Experience tells us that even the best plans will fall short of expectations if they're not deployed effectively. This means engaging everyone in the company in some way during planning and execution. The goal of a successful process is for everyone to see a clear link between the overall company direction and the work they perform.

You are encouraged to use the information in the *Manager's Guide to Business Planning* as a benchmark to compare your current practices. The tools and techniques you'll read about are tried and tested and are available for you to use as presented or to adapt to your unique situations.

Regardless of the industry or profit versus not-for-profit purpose of the business, I have defined what must happen from preparation for the planning process through the measurement of results. Planning in this context is not a single step, but a series of connected steps that lead you on the path to achieving your organization's goals.

The book follows the flow of the Four Ps of planning to help demonstrate the continuity required to move from planning to results.

Prepare

In this stage we cover the overall concept of planning, the ideas of collecting and analyzing data, and the structure of a plan. I will explain the relationship between strategic planning and business planning and how the two processes dovetail to provide long-term and short-term direction for the company. This is a complete guide to preparing a business plan that will serve as a baseline for future planning cycles. Another important aspect of preparation is the integration of the planning process throughout the company. You will find guidelines on how to do this effectively. Chapters 1 and 2 are dedicated to the preparation stage.

Plan

In this stage we cover performance planning, objectives, and measurements and finalizing the tools for execution. You will find detailed guidelines on linking company strategies to functional, departmental, and individual plans. If these linkages are missed or poorly aligned, there is a good chance of the dilution of overall results. In addition, I have explained a methodology for converting the *voice of the customer* (VOC) into clear measurements.

This will assist you in defining and delivering on customer requirements and ensuring a high degree of customer satisfaction. Several deployment tools, such as the Balanced Scorecard and Malcolm Baldrige Criteria for Excellence and the McKinsey 7 S Model are explained in detail. The tools referenced here will serve as ways to assess and organize the company goals, objectives, and strategies. They will also help every person gain a clear vision of the direction of the company. Chapters 3 and 4 are dedicated to providing this information.

Proceed

In this stage we cover moving forward by mobilizing the workforce to understand and execute the plan. I provide guidance on how to set up the business environment by establishing the right culture and communication systems. You'll read about a method for engaging people in the business cascade, coupled with the Strategy Deployment Worksheet to ensure that the information is documented.

Another essential aspect of moving forward is the review of the actual performance against the planned results. Detailed tracking and controlling guidelines are explained and include planning forms such as objective tracking and the Gantt chart. I present contingency planning as a method of making adjustments and coping successfully with changes in the external business environment. Chapters 5, 6, and 7 cover these topics.

Produce

In the final stage of the planning and execution process, we cover techniques for mastering learning. The information presented on learning focuses primarily on helping you learn faster than your competition as a way to create a sustainable advantage in the marketplace. I offer practical tips on effective planning best practices, as well as some of the traps to avoid during the planning and execution of plans. There is also a focus on how personal productivity enables the successful execution of plans. Chapters 8, 9, and 10 are dedicated to providing this information.

Finally, you'll also find an appendix at the end of the book with a planning toolkit that includes seven essential planning and problem-solving tools everyone should understand and know how to use.

Special Features

The idea behind the books in the Briefcase Books series is to give you practical information written in a friendly, person-to-person style. The chapters deal with both strategic and tactical issues and include lots of examples and how-to information. They also feature numerous sidebars designed to give you specific types of information you can use. Here are descriptions of the boxes you'll find in this book.

KEY TERM

Every subject has some special jargon, including this one, dealing with marketing and advertising. These boxes provide definitions of these terms and concepts.

SMART

MANAGING

These boxes do just what their name implies: give you tips and tactics for using the ideas in this book to intelligently manage and execute the planning process in your organization.

These boxes give you how-to hints on techniques insiders use to manage and execute the strategies and tactics described in this book.

It's always useful to have examples that show how the principles in the book are applied. These boxes provide descriptions of how managers and organizations have implemented the techniques in this book.

These boxes provide warnings for where things could go wrong when you're planning and implementing your planning process.

How can you make sure you won't make a mistake when you're trying to implement the techniques the book describes? You can't, but these boxes will give you practical advice on how to minimize the possibility of an error.

This icon identifies boxes where you'll find specific procedures or techniques you can follow to take advantage of the book's advice.

TOOLS

Acknowledgments

The daunting task of writing this book was made easier through a network of highly successful business managers who provided their insights, ideas, and working examples of how planning and execution are applied in the day-to-day business world. The biggest challenge in presenting information on planning and execution is to create a call to action where the examples, tools, and suggestions on their use will lead to the increase of actual results. I hope this view from the playing field will assist you in accomplishing this.

My special thanks to Bill Fruehauf, Jim McGeehin, Kerry Batchelder, John Shepherd, Mandy Henry, Gary Rosenfield, Ed Pignone, Bill Capezio, and Doreen Walker for their responsiveness and support that has helped bring this information to you.

Manager's Guide
to Business Planning

Fail to Plan ...
Plan to Fail

I n the words of the great UCLA basketball coach John Wooden, "In anything, failing to plan is planning to fail." The message he conveyed many years ago rings true today. Most busy managers focus more on the "what" of their efforts—the tangible results they are measured against. The emphasis lacking in many situations is on the "how" of their efforts, that being the plan to get there. In a global marketplace, the view of American managers is that they, for the most part, are fast on the implementation but lack the detailed planning process necessary to make their efforts successful. One European manager described it as "shooting from the hip." Irrespective of your own perception, the impact of poor planning on a business can result in such problems as false starts, waste and duplication, and dissatisfied customers.

Why Plan?

A manager in one of my client companies once commented, "Why plan? It only gets in the way of getting things done." Although this is a shortsighted view of planning, many managers believe that the value of planning is diminished because they must act more quickly, especially in competitive situations, and don't want to be held back by a list of objectives that are no longer realistic. Of course, this is a misconception that will be explored later, in that a good plan must have flexibility and contingencies to produce successful results.

It's important to dispel some of the myths regarding business planning to create a level playing field going forward. Exhibit 1-1 lists a few to ponder:

Myths	Facts
The planning process is busy work.	A good plan may be the only way to achieve your results in tough business conditions.
At the end of the day I am only measured on the bottom-line results.	The business plan is the roadmap to achieving and exceeding the expected results.
A business plan should follow a specified, structured format that is the same for all companies.	There are recommended formats that will help guide the planning process, but they should be customized to the needs and stage of business the company finds itself in (startup, growth, consolidation, etc.).
The plan should be prepared by the top leaders and passed down for implementation.	The most effective planning processes are two-way. Operating managers must have input into the goals and, certainly, the action plans.

Exhibit 1-1. The myths and facts of planning

To illustrate the point, consider the case of the man who wanted to cut back on his personal budget to save money this year. He planned to do his own gardening and yard work rather than hire a landscaper. One morning, he decided that he would trim a large tree in the yard. He climbed up the tree, sawing the branches below him. When he reached the top, he realized that he had cut off the only route back to the ground. Fortunately he was able to alert a neighbor, who came over with a ladder to rescue him. Just think how some basic planning could have eliminated the problem.

The Hierarchy of Business Planning

One way to think about planning for results is to envision the hierarchy or levels of planning that should occur in an organization, irrespective of its size, industry, or for-profit versus nonprofit. It might be helpful to see this planning as a hierarchy of thinking and ideas that come together to complete a picture. This becomes the vision of the future both in the long term (strategic plan) and in the short term (business plan). The third level is the planning for initiatives each year that will help drive both the long- and short-term priorities. Here is the hierarchy with some examples of each level.

Strategic Planning

The strategic planning process considers the external and internal impacts on the business, as well as looking at customers and markets to determine product and service fits. The resulting information combined with a competitive analysis leads to strategies that have the potential to grow the business and sustain profits over a long period (sustainability). This process is top-management-driven and feeds the

> **Strategic planning** An annual process designed to conduct an assessment of the business and to formulate a multi-year strategy, typically a three- to five-year window. **KEY TERM**

business planning process. The strategic plan is revisited every year to fine-tune assumptions and adjust to market conditions. The most successful companies use linking mechanisms to bridge from one stage of planning to the next. To link strategic and business planning, a strategy statement or summary of the strategic planning process is used to provide input into the business plan.

A medical device company in a highly competitive market used the expression for new product development, "First is first and second is last." This meant that they had to deliver new products to the market ahead of their competitors. During the strategic planning process, top management developed a product pipeline strategy that would unfold over several years. This information was passed down to key functions, such as R&D, product marketing, sales, purchasing, and manufacturing to incorporate into their business plans.

Business Planning

The business plan is completed by all department managers in profit centers and cost centers. The business plan focuses on how to achieve

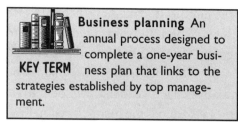

Business planning An annual process designed to complete a one-year business plan that links to the strategies established by top management.

revenue projections and fixed budget targets. The linking mechanism to bridge to departmental plans and business initiatives is the business plan document. It contains specific information regarding annual goals for revenue, profitability, etc., that can be used to complete detailed action plans.

A large manufacturing company developed a training program for managers called "Know the Numbers" in which all departmental managers where trained on the Profit and Loss Statement, including what was measured and how they could impact bottom-line numbers for their departments and overall company performance. One of the objectives of the training program was to create the mindset that managers were using the financial resources of the company as if they were writing checks from their personal checking accounts.

Functional/Departmental Plans and Business Initiative Planning

This is an annual planning process of functional/departmental plans and supporting initiatives that will directly impact the achievement of

THE FUNCTIONAL/ DEPART-MENTAL PLAN
The functional/departmental plan may have multi-year objectives in mind. In addition, a list of interdependencies should be created for communication and feedback prior to producing the final draft of the plan. This will encourage the preparation of joint objectives and sharing of resources. This is of particular importance if the plans are tied into bonus or other incentive programs.

business strategies and may have multi-year objectives in mind.

Although these plans and initiatives are prepared annually, a monthly reporting of progress against plans and initiatives is recommended for visibility to real-time performance. This creates opportunities for adjustments and corrections.

The Value of a Mission Statement in the Planning Scheme

Whether it's a company mission statement or at the functional or personal levels, the mission statement has enormous value in planning.

Creating a mission statement should not be considered an obligatory exercise. Your mission states the reasons you exist in the business. It should reflect the reason that your business opens its doors every day.

The mission should represent your commitment to the business and why you operate it.

When your mission statement represents and reflects your purpose it will attract and communicate to your customers and direct the work of employees. It can also provide a backdrop for decision making, asking the question, "Is this consistent with our mission?" With that in mind, ask yourself these questions:

> **SAMPLE MISSION STATEMENT**
> **Ben & Jerry's Ice Cream:** A product mission stated as: "To make, distribute, and sell the finest quality, all-natural ice cream and euphoric concoctions with a continued commitment to incorporating wholesome, natural ingredients and promoting business practices that respect the earth and the environment." This mission inspired Ben and Jerry to build a cause-related company.

- What is the purpose the entity serves for the business?
- How would you describe the output of your work process?
- Who are your target customers, both externally and internally?
- Who are your suppliers?

Recognizing the Uses of the Plan

In making the business case for using a business plan, it's important to delineate the purpose of the plan. Whether you're an executive who's responsible for building a business plan or a manager who's responsible for executing the plan, this principle will apply in the same way.

SMART MANAGING

WHAT'S IN IT FOR ME (WIIFM)

The main purpose of this plan is to make you more successful and your company more successful. In essence, it makes your job easier. Consider this an investment in You, Inc.: just as your plan is designed and executed, your personal value will increase. This investment will pay dividends over time as well. Once you've mastered the planning process, you will be able to repeat the cycle every time and improve on your personal best every year.

Purposes of the Plan

There are five purposes of business plans:

1. Determine where the company needs to go.
2. Determine the targets that will make the company successful.
3. Identify roadblocks and contingencies.
4. Keep the business on track to reach its targets.
5. Manage departmental and individual performance.

Planning to Fail—Biggest Mistakes to Avoid

It's estimated that less than half of all companies in the United States have business plans. The U.S. Department of Labor says that most companies that experience a major disaster will be out of business within five years. Yet only 25 percent of these companies have a disaster plan.

Mistakes to avoid:

1. Failure to develop solid timelines and measurements for the plan.
2. Failure to develop the supporting budget for the plan.
3. Failure to develop contingencies for roadblocks in the plan execution.
4. Failure to monitor progress at regular intervals.
5. Failure to communicate both good and bad news regarding business performance so mid-course corrections can be made.

Vista of Business Planning

In looking at planning as an interaction top-down process, this is the way you might view it as you watch it unfold.

Strategic View

Every company should conduct some type of strategic planning as a prelude to completing a business plan. This strategic view should include a vision for the future, a look at external impacts on the business, an assessment of target customers and product and service fit, a competitive analysis, an internal assessment of strengths and weaknesses, key strategies, and business goals. This information will feed the next phase of planning, which is the annual business plan.

> **PLAN TO PLAN**
>
> Think about the business year in advance of any formal planning sessions. Make notes on what went well and any missed expectations. This information will serve you well when you begin to put information on paper. You should store this information electronically so that your notes will become an audit trail from year to year. This is the essence of continuous improvement.

Company View

The responsibility of the top managers is to establish the overall company goals. These goals will emerge from the multi-year projections established in the strategic planning process.

Manager's View

The responsibility of the function or departmental managers is to give input into the overall company goals in terms of their mission and capabilities available to them. This should help to anchor the goals in terms of what is attainable with some stretching of resources. The view here is on operational planning and operational excellence.

Alignment

Alignment occurs when the strategies of the company are aligned with the business plan. The strategies create targets used to link executive through departmental levels, down to the individual employee levels. There should also be a cross-functional alignment between functions and departments to identify and clarify interdependencies and to assess the capabilities of shared services. The goals finalized in the business plan should be used to set department, team, and individual performance plans that can be monitored on a monthly and quarterly basis.

The Planning Process Model

Almost every process can be viewed as a closed system in which there are inputs, a process of action, and outputs that deliver a final product. This

ALIGNMENT QUESTIONS TO ASK

Are we structured to deliver the results? This will provide an opportunity to review the effectiveness of the structure of your current operations, with a focus on the most efficient people and methods of functioning. Do we have the necessary systems in place to achieve the results (communication, data management, etc.)? This will provide an opportunity to assess the current systems in place and determine if they're allowing you to gather more information quickly and accurately to support decision-making. Are the core business processes streamlined to add value to the customer? This will provide an opportunity to map and evaluate the effectiveness of core processes with an eye to eliminating waste and duplication. Have we identified interdependencies with other functions and departments? This will provide an opportunity to determine where your joint planning needs to occur.

model lends itself well to creating a planning tool and mental model for any manager to use in either high-level or tactical planning. In its most practical format, it would look like Exhibit 1-2 for your own planning effort. In the application of this model, you will add and delete as your specific function dictates. This list will be converted into specific measurements in Chapter 3.

SAMPLE BUSINESS PROCESS MODEL

Typical Inputs

- A description of the business in terms of industry focus, products and services, and markets served.
- A set of Key Results Areas (KRAs) and specific business objectives for the coming business year.
- Mission statement that defines the purpose of the company, function, or department, and what results you're striving for.
- Actual performance versus plan on key indicators such as revenue and budget.
- Forecast for volume of products and/or services (obtained from voice of the customer and other projections).
- A list of all potential operational improvements that will make the business more competitive.
- Staffing forecast based on the above data.
- Supplier feedback regarding pricing for the next business year.

Typical Processes

- Reviewing the data inputs and thinking about and analyzing what has been presented.
- Reviewing, refining, and creating a working document.

Exhibit 1-2. Inputs, processes, and outputs of the the business process model (continued on next page)

- Establishing the right performance standards and measurements for each of the objectives.
- Setting realistic and challenging objectives for each of the KRAs.
- Analyzing the projections and creating final numbers for the plan.
- Identifying the levels of staffing and total compensation (salary and benefits) for both full-time and part-time employees.
- Identifying the right improvement that will have the most impact on the business, short-term.
- Identifying any increases or decreases in the cost of doing business with suppliers.

Typical Outputs
- Expected costs from suppliers.
- Solidify the direction and purpose served by this business and support functions.
- Working document to support future planning.
- Agreed-on KRAs.
- Agreed-on objectives.
- Agreed-on final numbers.
- Projected staffing plan and costs for the business year.
- A final list of operation improvements (not more than five) that will improve productivity.

Exhibit 1-2. Continued

Planning to Plan: Collecting Data to Feed Your Plan

Gathering data from your customers and suppliers will provide an excellent perspective on how well the company, business unit, or department has performed during the past year. This data will allow you to set more accurate goals for performance based on the strengths and weaknesses uncovered in the feedback. This procedure involves forecasting the future by asking questions of your key constituencies. No manager has a crystal ball to tell exactly what will happen and when. Forecasting and listening to the voice of customers, suppliers, and your employees will be as close to seeing the future as you can get. Use the following suggestions to begin the data collection. Include any other critical interfaces that will have an impact on your plan. Here is a survey you can use to forecast customer needs and buying patterns.

Own the Customer's Total Experience

The goal of collecting this information is to determine how you can create a total customer experience. This involves creating a satisfying experience for the customer at every touch point and in every interaction the customer may have with a company representative. This information will help to shore up those touch points and interactions.

FORECASTING CUSTOMER NEEDS AND BUYING PATTERNS

What is your current level of satisfaction with the following, on a scale of 1–10, and why did you give that rating?
(10 = Extremely High, 5 = Moderate, 1 = Extremely Low)

TOOLS

- Quality of products/services used? Do they perform to specifications? _____

  Why did you give this rating? _____

- Reliability of products/services used? Do they deliver the same or better quality each time? _____

  Why did you give this rating? _____

- Ease of contact? _____

  Why did you give this rating? _____

- Responsiveness of the company representatives to resolve issues? _____

  Why did you give this rating? _____

- List any specific issues you would like to be resolved. _____

  _____

- What one recommendation would you make to raise your scores?

  _____

- How do you compare our overall performance to our competitors? (Best, Better, Equal, Worse) _____

  Why did you give this rating? _____

- What is your future plan to purchase our products/services? (Increase, Stay at Current Levels, Decrease) _____

Survey Scoring

Scores of 8 to 10 for each question are a strong indicator that they can be counted on for repeat purchases; other scores represent some satisfaction, neutral, or dissatisfied customers. Use the comments to make critical improvements if you want to be able to depend on their revenues over time.

Use the input regarding future purchases to determine where there are opportunities for up-selling and cross-selling of your products/services. This may help to determine if your revenues will increase, stay flat, or decrease in the coming year.

Forecasting Supplier Capabilities and Costs

The information gained in conversations with suppliers is especially valuable to support functions that are often referred to as cost centers. The questions you will want to ask focus on three key metrics: (1) cost of materials (raw, subassembly, or finished) and services, (2) quality of materials and services, and (3) speed at which the materials and services are delivered to the company.

QUESTIONS FOR SUPPLIERS

SMART

MANAGING

Cost
- Do you anticipate cost increases or reductions during this business year?
- What specific cost reduction programs are currently being used to control costs?
- Do you currently have the capacity to handle an increase in orders of 10 to 20%?

Quality
- What specific programs (Lean, SPC, etc.) do you currently employ or plan to implement that will ensure the quality (conformance to specifications and reliability) over the next two years?
- Do you have a program for assessing and selecting subcontractors so that we can be sure that our expectations are met?

Speed
- What process improvements or continuous improvements are being made to decrease turnaround times and increase shipping speed or materials and services?
- What do you need from our company to make these improvements?

Benchmarking

Use benchmarking for identification of "best practices" to establish attainable goals and targets for improvement, especially important in competitive situations.

WHAT SHOULD BE BENCHMARKED?

SMART

MANAGING

- Key Business Drivers
- Sales per Employee
- Costs vs. Industry Averages
- Product Margins for Comparable Products
- Order Fulfillment Rates (accept, process, fill, ship, deliver)

Using This Data

As Peter Drucker once stated, "Information by itself is useless unless you do something with it." Acting on this advice, the next steps will provide a guide for creating action with your information.

FOR EXAMPLE

PROFIT AND COST CENTERS

Both profit centers and cost centers are critical to the success of every business. Profit centers include sales, marketing, and manufacturing. Cost centers include finance, human resources, purchasing, and information technology. These functions may also be referred to as shared services. In the planning process, many companies now use the concept of zero-based budgeting, in which each year is planned with a blank sheet of paper, rather than using the past year's performance and just adjusting the numbers. Zero-based budgeting requires a more complete analysis to arrive at a final determination of what the most accurate forecast is for the coming year.

Analyzing the Information

Increasing your ability to analyze large amounts of information and make accurate assumptions and decisions with this information will be critical to the planning process. One of the biggest gaps in the planning process for busy managers is the need to create shortcuts to getting at and analyzing information for the business plan. The old saying in the information management world, "Garbage in, garbage out" definitely applies in this situation. Without an accurate foundation and potentially faulty assumptions, the profitability of the business is at risk.

Evaluate Your Analytic Skills

Exhibit 1-3 is a worksheet designed to assist in identifying strengths and development needs.

Bringing the Data Together

After you've collected the data, the next step is to summarize and synthesize it so that it can be used to complete both a business plan and a functional/departmental plan. You'll be able to use the planning tools presented in Chapters 4 and 5 to arrange the data in formats and templates that will provide a clearer picture of what the data points represent. To be successful, you'll need to identify and test your assumptions. When

SEEKING FEEDBACK

To ensure that your evaluation is accurate, ask for feedback from your boss, peers, and subordinates in terms of their perceptions of your skill level. One method of obtaining feedback is to seek out a trusted peer and ask this person to give you their honest opinion of your analytical skills as described in this short assessment. If there are any shortcomings, this person may act as a sounding board for you in the future as you work on a particular skill area.

you've reached a preliminary conclusion about a particular issue, test your assumptions and conclusions with others, including your staff, peers, and immediate manager. You'll need to be open to new or opposing points of view to determine the best course of action. You may want to capture the various viewpoints in writing so that you can reflect on the information.

Planning meetings are effective in synthesizing data but require pre-planning and preparation prior to a decision-making meeting. Specify the type of meeting you want others to participate in and define the specific

Strengths	S	M	D	Specific On-the-Job Examples
Business Acumen Know the vision and strategies of the business				
Know the financial measures, both macro (overall business) and micro (business unit)				
Analytical Skills Approach work from a systematic point of view				
See the connections and interrelationships in data				
Identify the underlying assumptions in the data and test your assumptions with others				
Use analytical tools versus "gut feel"				

Exhibit 1-3. Evaluating your analytical skills. **Rating:** S = Strength; M = Meets Expected Level; D = Development Opportunity

topic, objectives, and meeting outline prior to bringing people together. For example, an information-sharing meeting would be facilitated differently than an input meeting or decision-making meeting. Be sure to share information in advance of the meeting whenever possible to eliminate time needed during the meeting for a first-time review of any data points. There is more information to help improve meeting management in Chapter 10 on personal productivity techniques.

Apply Your Financial Knowledge

The need for managers to apply financial thinking to their plans is becoming increasingly important. This knowledge needs to go beyond the traditional mentality of controlling expenses into identifying ways to increase productivity that impact the bottom line of the business. Think about this in terms of increasing profits versus cutting costs. One of the risks of cost cutting is reduced service to the customer and potential loss of customers and revenues. Here are a few suggestions to explore during the planning process.

> **FOR EXAMPLE**
> **REDUCING DISCRETIONARY SPENDING**
> A technology company that depends heavily on computers to run its business reviewed all its maintenance contracts for service and repair of their computers. They were able to reduce the maintenance costs substantially by renegotiating contracts and then establishing a small in-house response team who eliminated many expensive service calls by performing routine maintenance and problem-solving.

1. Look at both variable and fixed costs for opportunities to reduce costs without downgrading service levels.
2. What are the top four to five costly items in your profit and loss statement? How can you work on them for the coming year?
3. In reviewing your top four to five suppliers, is it possible to consolidate to half that number and still maintain service levels? The idea is to go deeper with a few suppliers and build partnerships for the long term.

The Planning Window

The business planning cycle or planning window may vary from business to business, especially when the planning year starts and finishes at different times during the calendar year. For example, the U.S. federal government planning cycle runs from October 1 through September 30. In a calendar year planning cycle, the strategic plan is in the June timeframe so that it can drive the annual business plan later in August. This information, in turn, can feed the budgeting process in November so that everything can be completed for the new business year beginning in January. Performance reviews and objectives for the new business are completed in December and January, which may include bonus or other incentive compensation based on business results. In addition, quarterly business reviews are conducted to track progress against the plans.

Exhibit 1-4 shows a typical planning cycle. It tracks with a calendar year but is easily scalable to any annual planning cycle.

Hitting the Sweet Spot Between Planning and Execution

The "sweet spot" on a baseball bat is the unique position on the bat that makes the ball fly the farthest. A similar spot exists on a tennis racket or golf club.

The same is true of the planning and execution challenge. The failure to execute a plan fully or well results in limited success. This may mean missed targets or opportunities that will give a company the momentum it needs to sustain itself over the next planning period or beyond.

The application to this example becomes clearer when we look at what actually occurs after a business plan is completed. The plan should become a working document for both the overall company reporting and departmental action. The missing piece, or the sweet spot, is the linchpin to couple the plan and the actions required to achieve it. In order to make

---

Execution The completion of the steps required to reach a specific objective. Remember, an A+ plan that is poorly executed will be outperformed by a well-executed B+ strategy every time. *Execution: The Discipline of Getting Things Done* by **KEY TERM** Lawrence Bossidy and Ram Charan provides an excellent perspective on a Fortune 500 approach to execution. One of my favorite quotes from the book illustrates this point, "I saw leadership place too much emphasis on what some called high level strategy, on intellectualizing and philosophizing and not enough on implementation. People would agree on a project or an initiative and then nothing would come of it."

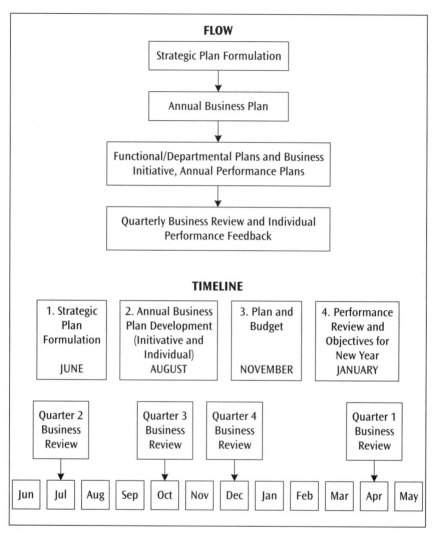

Exhibit 1-4. Typical planning cycle

this seamless, a formal bridge must be built to move into the execution or implementation phase.

We will explore this in detail in Chapters 4 and 6 so that this will become failsafe each business year.

Creating the Right Mindset Going Forward

Successful planning requires both the commitment and the skills to be effective. This means that you must have the right mindset regarding

NEW ROCHELLE PUBLIC
LIBRARY

User name: PETERS,
AUDEN M

Payment date: 6/4/2015,
12:15

Title: From the plantation
to the penitentiary [CD]
Item ID: 31019155001848

Title: Eleven rings [CD
audiobook] : the soul of
success
Item ID: 31019155669271

Amount Previously Due:
Total: $2.60

Payment status:
Payment type:
Amount paid: $2.60

Remaining balance: $0.00

your understanding of the business and combine this with a mix of function/technical excellence, planning, and action. Here are some suggestions on how to build the right mindset going forward.

Increasing Your Functional/Technical Excellence

What Excellence Looks Like: Individuals at the excellence level have expert knowledge and understanding of their main functional areas of responsibility. They keep abreast of new developments and industry trends as well as impart new ideas in the function, department, or work unit. They are technology-proficient in running all aspects of their functions.

Quick Tips

- Join professional organizations where you can meet other professionals in your field and use this opportunity to share ideas or conduct informal benchmarking on areas such as processes, procedures, and technology infusion. There may be an opportunity to hear guest speakers on current topics that may provide a source of continuing education.
- Read and research using both textbooks and Internet searches to get the latest thinking or developments in your field. Business journals and industry-specific newsletters and magazines are also excellent sources of real-time information that can be shared with your staff and peers.

Increasing Your Planning Competence

What Excellence Looks Like: Individuals who are competent in planning understand the big picture and integrate this knowledge to accurately assess the scope of projects and plans and are able to set realistic goals and objectives. In addition, they are able to complete the detail work by breaking it down into process steps, which include schedules and tasks. They are also able to anticipate problems and obstacles. Finally, they measure progress against objectives and evaluate the results.

> **Planning** The establishment of the targets to be achieved at a future point in time. Remember, a plan is a **KEY TERM** formal document designed to establish the targets to be achieved. Without effective planning, the actions that are taken and ensuing results may be diminished. We have learned that our behavior is goal-directed and that a well-developed plan has potential to drive that behavior forward.

Quick Tips

- Make an effort to understand the strategy and major objectives of the business and how you can impact them.
- Establish planning time. It's difficult to crystallize a plan without adequate time to time it through. Avoid "planning on the fly."
- Find another departmental manager in your company who you feel has expertise in conceptualizing a plan and can create supporting action plans. Review his/her work products and use them as examples of a best practice in your company.

Increasing Your Bias for Action

What Excellence Looks Like: Action-oriented individuals enjoy working hard. They are energized by taking on challenges and solving problems. They are able to apply the correct amount of planning to get the required results and can seize opportunities when they arise.

Quick Tips

- Become a more effective daily, weekly, and monthly action planner. Make to-do lists and evaluate the results every day. Learn how to better set priorities among competing tasks.
- Increase your speed of action by getting more done each day. Evaluate your use of available technology (phone, Internet/e-mail, face-to-face, etc.) and determine how you can increase your speed of communication and decision making. Look for time wasters and eliminate them.
- Fail falling forward. Don't procrastinate; take moderate risks and learn from the mistakes. Risk should not be an inhibitor to action.

Manager's Checklist for Chapter 1

- ☑ Identify your role in the business planning process.
- ☑ Compare your mission statement to the benchmark.
- ☑ Understand the planning process cycle and timeline.
- ☑ Use tips on how to collect and analyze data to improve overall planning and increase results.

☑ Establish a planning window that fits your business situation.

☑ Create the right mindset to be an effective planner.

☑ Look for opportunities to improve your planning skills.

Chapter

2

Creating a Focused Business Plan

A s we discussed in Chapter 1, the business plan is the centerpiece of the planning process. It links the longer-term view of strategic planning to the tactical or annual plans for business units, functions, departments and teams, and individuals.

Three Paths to Take

For startup companies that are in the early stages of building a business:

Business Plan ➜ Operating and Financial Plans

For companies that have been in business and have a track record of documented performance:

Strategic Plan ➜ Business Plan ➜ Functional/Departmental Operating Plans

Or

Strategic Plan ➜ Functional/Departmental Operating Plans

It's interesting to note that many functional/departmental managers have never been tasked with creating a business plan. The main reason for this is that they have primarily been tasked with focusing on their areas of function as part of an overall plan for the company. In some respects, this may be limiting for them, especially if they're asked to develop a plan for a new line of business.

The business plan will serve both the outside and inside planning and communication needs for the company. The outside value is for investors and customers to have visibility to the game plan of the company so that they can gain confidence in the company's ability to achieve its results.

Focusing the Business Plans

It's important to identify the main focus of a business plan because it will help to determine what to include and emphasize.

Startup-focused plans identify the steps that a new business will follow to create products, services, and customers. It will use the standard topics including the company, product or service, market, forecasts, strategy, implementation milestones, management team, and financial analysis. The financial analysis includes projected sales, profit and loss, balance sheet, and cash flow—all critical aspects of creating the initial game plan.

Internally focused plans are not intended for outside investors, banks, or other third parties. They might exclude information that's not relevant to internal plans, such as the company background, ownership information, etc., while including only those areas of the essential components that apply to their key strategies and business objectives. One example of an internally focused plan is one that emphasizes operations and focuses on internal capabilities. This type of plan is more detailed on specific implementation milestones, dates, deadlines, and responsibilities of functions that support the overall business.

Growth-focused plans will emphasize the opportunities that may exist for new product lines, acquiring another business, or creating a major expansion of the existing business. Quite often, these plans are linked to financial requirements and/or investment opportunities. For example, an acquisition plan would require a complete assessment of the acquired business and projected costs of acquisition and operation on the overall financials of the current business. This is especially important if investment capital is required.

Viability-focused plans are essentially startup plans that include the essentials of the business plan presented here with emphasis on the information being presented to help determine if the new venture has the return on investment necessary to move forward.

Essential Components of a Business Plan

The categories contained in a business plan will vary slightly based on the type and focus of the plan as mentioned above. The components referenced next can be used for both external and internal planning purposes. The operations section will provide guidance on how to convert this information into a day-to-day approach to more detailed plans needed to drive the business forward each year.

Executive Summary: An Introduction and Overview for This Business

In this section the focus is on the foundation of the company. Relevant information presented here should include:

- Type of business and markets served.
- Date of incorporation and business structure (corporation, sole proprietorship, LLC, etc.), publicly or privately held.
- Main objectives of the business (why it's in business, what it's in business to do).
- Advantages over the competition, if applicable.
- Contact information, including web address.

FOR EXAMPLE

SAMPLE EXECUTIVE SUMMARY

Introduction

Value Added Resources is a global consulting firm committed to helping companies increase their overall business performance by providing the resources required to solve difficult problems and meet the challenges of shifting market demand. The company serves multiple market segments, with a focus on heath care.

Objectives

1. Provide value-added services that enhance client business performance and results.
2. Have a client retention rate of 70% by end of first year.
3. Become an established regional resource within two years of market entry.
4. Participate in community activities and provide low-cost services to small-business startups.

Keys to Success

- Superior customer service.

- Convenience: offer users a wide range of business services in one environment.
- Reputation: credibility, integrity, and 100% dedication.
- Seasoned consulting team.
- Maintain low overhead and expenses.

Company Summary: Ownership and Startup Plan

For startup situations especially, this is an opportunity to showcase the background and unique skills of the founders and key managers of the company. In addition to this background information, a short description of the startup plan should be included. The depth of this summary may depend on whether or not investors or

BUSINESS PURPOSE

"The purpose of business is to attract and maintain customers," concludes Peter Drucker. This concise view of why you're in business will help to focus the information included in the business plan. Ultimately, the business plan must create value for the customer as well as provide a return on investment to other stakeholders such as employees, stockholders, and investors. In addition, the information presented in the business plan will be used for more detailed planning by functional managers.

lenders will be primary recipients of this document. This section should also include the projected amount of startup cash required for the major expenses associated with the startup period.

THE BRAIN DRAIN

Ideas for new products and services can come from a number of sources, including customer focus groups, marketing, research and development, and company employees. One company used a multi-level brainstorming meeting to encourage creativity and innovation to come up with ideas for new products. The Brain Drain made use of creative thinking techniques, subgroup design time, and poster sessions to build on the ideas. Sessions were held in several company locations, each time building on the ideas of the previous sessions. A final consolidation meeting was the last step in bringing a product idea to the drawing board to test feasibility. Several new products were developed through this process.

Products and Services: Detailed Explanation of the Products and Services Mix

In this section you want to display your range of products and services and how they're positioned to serve current and future market segments. This may be done by using a matrix to show current and future plans to deliver your products and services (Exhibit 2-1). This matrix will help to organize the data presented here. This is not intended to be a marketing plan. That will come later during the detailed planning process when functional plans are prepared.

	Current Markets and Customers Served/ Expected Revenues	**New Markets and Customers to Be Served/Expected Revenues**
Current Products and Services		
New Products and Services		

Exhibit 2-1. Matrix for analyzing products and services mix

Market Analysis: Market Description and How Products and Services Fit With Customer Needs

In this section it's important to gain visibility as to who your target customers are. This can be a listing by market segment. For each listing, identify the customer needs and wants that you will fulfill (Exhibit 2-2). This should provide insights into how well this fit is working. In addition, list the reasons that customers choose to buy from you or the value proposition that underpins your success as a company.

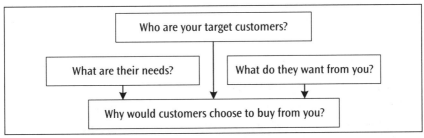

Exhibit 2-2. Analyzing customer needs that you can fulfill

Strategy Implementation: Major Strategies and Expected Results

This section should contain a description of the company's high-level strategies and expected results. It would also be helpful to create a short list of competitors' strengths and weaknesses to be used in developing selling and customer strategies. The strategies should center around how to maintain and grow market share, financial objectives regarding revenues and profits, and customer satisfaction measures such as retention rates and evaluations of product/service quality and reliability.

Strategies should be created with deployment in mind. These high-level strategies will serve as a planning platform for both functional plans and deployment programs such as the Balanced Score. These programs and tools will be discussed in detail in Chapter 5.

Strategic priorities should fit into these major categories:

Financial

- **Targets:** Revenue, Gross Margin, Operating Income, Return on Net Assets (RONA)
- **Priorities include:** Meet targets for revenues, operating income, return on net assets, and earnings per share (if publicly traded)

Customer

- **Targets:** % Retained, % Market Share, % Satisfied Customers (survey results)
- **Priorities include:** Increase retention rates, increase satisfaction measures, increase market share

Products and Services

- **Targets:** Number of New Product Introductions, % Defects, Market Position
- **Priorities include:** Increase new product introductions, improve quality, and maintain industry position of first or second in every brand/product line

People

- **Priorities include:** Reduce turnover and increase retention rates

Internal Capabilities (Core Capabilities)

- **Targets:** % Processes Reengineered, % Productivity Increases
- **Priorities include:** Process management efficiency and productivity increases

The competitor analysis should include:

What are they best at?

- Factors enhancing their bargaining power (e.g., buyers and suppliers)
- Factors that insulate them from competition
- Greater scale of assets, market share
- Strong implementation ability for new services
- Abundance of resources and skill

Where are they weak?

- Factors worsening their bargaining power (e.g., buyers and suppliers)
- Factors that expose them to threats from competitors
- Smaller scale of assets, market share
- Weaker implementation ability for new services
- Lack of resources and skill
- What aspects of their business weaknesses can you leverage to drive your business strategy? This information can form the basis of a competitive strategy in which you are leveraging your strengths against the competitor's weaknesses.

Strategy Sample

1. Medical Device Company
2. Introduce new, differentiated products ahead of the competition
3. Defend existing products (market share, profitability)
4. Increase product quality, exceeding industry standards
5. Initiate cost reduction programs that increase margins and reduce expenses

---

THE VITAL FEW

"You see, regardless of the size of the company, no company can afford everything it would like to do. Resources have to be allocated. The essence of strategic planning is to allocate resources to those areas that have the greatest future potential." Reginald Jones, *Making Strategy Work*. The quote speaks to the real objective of the planning process: to reach those vital few strategies that can be activated and achieved in a one- to three-year period. The problem that exists in many companies is the proliferation of strategies and the danger of diluting their successful execution because of the sheer volume and resource requirements.

Annual Operating Plan

The emphasis in this section is on the supply chain for the preparation, assembly, manufacture, and delivery of your products and services. The information presented here will again allow for more detailed planning by managers who represent the subfunctions such as engineering, purchasing, inventory management, quality control, operations/manufacturing, and logistics. The key areas to be covered are:

- **Equipment:** Describe the equipment required to run the business. This will include the value of existing equipment and projected costs of additional equipment needs.
- **Capital Asset Management:** Provide expectations regarding inventory management, days sales outstanding, and receivables/payables balance. Create a complete list of assets.
- **Materials Management:** Identify supplier requirements in terms of price, lead times, and cost. Look for opportunities to build long-term relationships with suppliers.
- **Production:** Identify production cycle times and production rates per product line. In service situations, map processes and identify opportunities to streamline. Consider the measurements of cost, quality, and speed of delivery.
- **Quality:** Provide specifications and standards that are expected to be attained in the production and use of products and services. You'll want to include customer satisfaction measurements, as well.
- **Facilities, Plant, and Office Space:** Describe the facilities and premises including the square footage and locations of each facility. It may be useful to include drawings

> **Operational planning**
> The day-to-day implementation of policies, practices, and systems that are consistent with the mission and that support the overall company strategic objectives. The overall goal of operational planning is to provide specific information regarding company-wide imperatives such as cost reduction, cost management requirements, functional priorities, and higher-level metrics that can help guide detail planning at both the department and individual levels. As was stated earlier, alignment is the litmus test in which goals are integrated in some way at every level of the organization.
>
> **KEY TERM**

of the building, copies of lease agreements, and/or recent real estate appraisals. The total value of the land and buildings required for business operations should be calculated, including overall worth of the bricks and mortar.

- **Cost:** Give direction to support and production and delivery units by estimating the standard cost of products and services.

E-Commerce Strategy: How the Company Will Maintain a Presence on the Internet

In this section you'll explain how you'll conduct business through the Internet, if applicable. In every situation, it will be important to maintain a website to have a method of introducing the company. In addition, a description of products and services and a method of contacting key personnel at the company will provide a basic connection to the company. One opportunity to take advantage of is to use some of the information in the business plan to populate the website. If you choose to sell products and services from your website, an e-commerce section can be built in, including credit cards for payment.

Management Team Summary

In this section you'll want to include each key member of the company management team, their qualifications, their accomplishments, and their commitments to the business success. This information is especially valuable for investors and customers as they determine whether they will do business with the company. This information offers a degree of credibility for the management of the company, so it should be prepared with careful details and projections of strong leadership skills.

Financials

Since finance is considered by many as the language of business, this section is critical to the startup and day-to-day management of the company. The information presented here will be integrated with overall reporting of company financial results, and will provide specifics to the subfunctions of the company to set their annual goals.

The centerpieces of this information are the profit and loss/income statement and the balance sheet.

Total Revenues
− Cost of Goods Sold

Gross Margin
− Operating Expenses

Income Before Taxes and Interest (IBTI)
− Taxes and Interest

Net Income (or Loss)

Exhibit 2-3. The basic components of an income statement

Assets
Current Assets (receivables, inventory, cash on hand, etc.)
+ Long-Term Assets (plant and equipment)
= Total Assets

Liabilities
Current Liabilities (payables, short-term debt)
+ Long-Term Equity (stock, shareholder equity, etc.)
= Total Liabilities

Exhibit 2-4. The basic components of a balance sheet

Dealing with Different Personalities

During the planning process, there will be many opportunities to share and discuss information as it's finalized into the business plan. Personal preferences and personalities will have an impact on the success of these interactions by determining how conflicts and differing points of view are resolved. There are several personality styles assessments and indicators, such as the Myers-Briggs Type Indication (MBTI), Activity Vector Analysis, and DISC.

It's advisable to engage in a discussion of similar and different styles at the senior management levels, using one of these tools as an awareness vehicle. Becoming aware of the various styles that exist in a planning team may help to encourage better cooperation and communication identifying strengths and gaps in the team. It may also help the team to recognize their diverse approaches, from big picture (Intuitive in MBTI) to detailed focus (Sensing in MBTI), and ensure that attention is given to all perspectives during the planning process.

Functional and Departmental Plan Development

Almost every process can be viewed as a closed system in which there are inputs, a process of action, and outputs that deliver a final product. This model lends itself well to creating a planning tool and mental model for any manager to use in either high-level or tactical planning. In its most practical format, it would look like an outline of your planning effort. In the application of this model, you'll add and delete as your specific function dictates. This outline will be converted into specific measurements in Chapter 4.

TRICKS OF THE TRADE

TEAM EXERCISE: THREE SYMBOLS

Ask each team member to draw three symbols on a piece of paper: a circle, a square, and a triangle. Next, ask them to rank the symbols from 1 to 3, where 1 represents their problem-solving style most and 3 the least. After the ranking is completed ask for a show of hands of who had the circle as 1. Explain that the circle represents a holistic approach to problem solving. Next ask how many had the square as 1. Explain that the square represents a focused approach to problem solving. Next, ask how many had the triangle as 1. Explain that the triangle represents an analytical approach to problem solving. The message is that this team represents a diversity of thinking and problem solving. Some may prefer to discuss the big picture first, while others will want to dive into the details immediately. And, of course, some may be comfortable with a combined approach. A successful planning team will make an effort to work with all problem-solving approaches, finding that different styles can be complementary to achieving a strong final result.

Building Functional Plans

There are several ways to build the functional plans. In this example we will build from the framework established in Chapter 1.

Applying the Input-Process-Output Model to Functional Plan Development

Inputs

- A description of the business in terms of industry focus, products and services, and markets served

Process

- Review each section of the business plan to identify impacts on your area of responsibility.
- Identify a supporting mission statement for your area of responsibility.
- Identify the key results that will be required to meet day-to-day operations and to help achieve the strategies and objectives of the company.
- Solidify the direction and purpose served by this business and support functions.
- Begin to develop the framework for a specific operating plan.

Outputs

- Sample key results areas (KRAs) for the functional plans:
  - R&D.
  - Launch new products ahead of the competition.
  - Reduce cycle times.
- Sales
  - Achieve revenue goals.
  - Create customer retention program.
- Operations
  - Meet production goals.
  - Improve customer satisfaction for on-time delivery of products and services.
- Engineering
  - Improve product and service quality.
  - Support reduction of cycle times.
- Finance
  - Provide financial analysis tools, turnaround reports, and timely information required to track and measure business performance (monthly, quarterly, annually).
- Purchasing
  - Increase supplier quality.
  - Reduce lead times for raw and finished goods.
- Human Resources
  - Ensure proper talent is acquired (right skills and motivation) to meet business plan requirements.

- ■ Information Technology
  - • Provide support for software development to meet information reporting needs.
  - • Provide on-site problem-solving support via company-managed help desk.
- ■ Safety
  - • Reduce lost-time accidents.
  - • Expand safety awareness programs to every department in the company.

Sample Functional Plan Format: Focus on Part 1

The information presented in Chapter 1 regarding the development of a mission statement and the information gleaned from your business plan will provide the input for completing the first part of the functional plan. Use the following format as a guide to using the information presented in this book.

FUNCTIONAL AREA

Mission Statement:

Part 1
- ■ Key Results Areas

TOOLS

Part 2
- ■ Objectives
- ■ Maintenance
- ■ Improvement
- ■ Other

Part 3
- ■ Organization and Human Resource Plans
- ■ Link to Annual Budgets

Part 4
- ■ Performance Standards and Measurements Established

Part 5
- ■ How Tracked

Integrating Plans

In most business operations, discrete functions emerge after startup that are required to run the business effectively. Each of these functions

---

CREATING MOMENTUM FOR BUSINESS PLANNING

The idea of participating in a planning session often evokes visions of boredom and just plain old lack of enthusiasm. One way to create momentum for the planning session is for the company leaders to emphasize the importance of participation and that they are counting on every employee's input for the company to be successful in a given business year.

Some examples of creating momentum are: publish the planning calendar well in advance, prepare departmental managers with worksheets and planning tools, provide opportunities for brainstorming sessions to gather data and share ideas during the planning process, create updates and communications that place importance on the planning process and the end results, and use town hall meetings to create motivation and participation in helping to shape the direction of the company.

---

will produce an individual plan in support of the overall company business plan and strategies. One danger that exists in all businesses is the planning-in-a-vacuum risk, in which an individual function or department plans in isolation and lacks an integration point with other parts of the business. This is often true where a business has become interdependent in all aspects of its functions in order to be successful in reaching its goals. There are two key integration points that will be addressed: horizontal and vertical. When these integrations are completed, the likelihood of business success in a given year increases and the company achieves an important step in alignment.

Horizontal Integration

The first integration that should occur prior to the finalization of the functional plan is a planning session that involves cross-functional representatives, often unit managers, to share preliminary key results areas and objectives. The identification of interdependencies with the other functions required for successful overall business plan achievement is discussed. An important takeaway here is the agreement on shared responsibility for achieving results.

Vertical Integration

The second integration is within the function, from top to bottom. Again, sharing the key results areas and objectives will ensure that each team member has a clear understanding of the direction of the functional plan and will be able to use this information to finalize their individual performance plans. This is a valuable input opportunity in which feedback regarding the positioning of the key results areas and objectives will help to fine-tune the final plan. This also creates a buy-in to the achievement of the plan in support of the company business plan.

One method of integration is called Hoshin Kanri or Catchball. This technique is part of the Japanese Hoshin Planning process and will be discussed in Chapter 5 to assist in the deployment of these plans.

How Catchball Works

The idea is centered around moving or throwing a ball to various parts of the organization. The ball represents the major goals of the organization and can be used to develop more detailed plans as the ball is passed throughout the organization.

Exhibit 2-5. The Catchball process

At the end of the Catchball process, the management team has received feedback from its functions and confirmed the viability of its key goals. As the feedback loop is closed here, the information is passed down to the next level for more detailed planning and confirmation. This becomes the deployment point for action plans, which are linked to the top of the organization.

SMART

MANAGING

FUSION

A lot has been written regarding the seamless or boundaryless organization, in which the information and processes cross the organization smoothly, which ultimately adds value to the customer.

The problem that occurs in typical organizations is the "silo" effect, where each function or entity becomes its own silo in which processes and information can be self-contained to the detriment of productivity.

The idea of fusion is at the heart of creating the seamless organization. Roundtable meetings designed to share information in the early stages of business planning will help to break down the silos and create a more open environment for joint goal setting and measurement.

Putting It All Together

Order and efficiency versus chaos and complexity are the yin and yang of creating successful organizations in today's dynamic business environment. David Freedman explores these ideas in his *Harvard Business Review* article, "Is Management Still a Science?" Several researchers have tried to lay out the ground rules for efficiency and order for the successful industrial organization, but the reality is that chaos and complexity have become the major challenge today. Planning fits this scenario quite well, however, considering that having the roadmap serves as a launch point for real-time decision making and adjustments. The business plan may be one of the most important tools in dealing with change. If the plan is truly aligned, large-scale adjustments can be made quickly and smoothly to help the organization navigate though the white waters of chaos and complexity. The business plan may act as the rudder in the process.

Mini Case Study: Spiro-Gyro, Inc.

Long ago, in a faraway corner of the galaxy, Spiro-Gyro, a small company that created and manufactured gyros, became a big company. This company was founded and managed by one man. From the day the company began, he designed its gyros, oversaw their manufacture, and was personally involved in the details of the entire operation.

With the passage of time, the company's reputation became legend throughout the universe, for its gyros were the best. So creating, making, and selling these gyros became the company's most important responsibility.

As the demand for more gyros grew and grew, more people were needed to make and sell them and to create better and better ones. In fact an entire department was created to do nothing but search the galaxy and to hire, hire, hire.

The phenomenal demand for gyros required new and efficient manufacturing processes. The increased number of employees made communications more challenging, and the company's ever-increasing growth demanded financial control. Differentiated functions soon emerged, led by some who had risen through the ranks and by aliens who joined the company from distant planets.

The company's success rested primarily on a function called Genesis. The people who inhabited this mysterious realm were special, for it was their job to create new gyros. Another major function was called Prometheus. The people in Prometheus made the gyros that the people in Genesis created. A third major function was called Ulysses. The people in Ulysses traveled the galaxy, selling the gyros in far corners of the universe. As the company grew, a fourth function emerged called Rhinegold, wherein rested responsibility for the company's finances.

There also emerged a set of support functions called Felicitations that were responsible for providing shared services to the company such as information management, employee relations, safety, and legal advice. The people in Felicitations did not create, make, or sell gyros, nor did they generate capital to do so. Yet in countless ways they assisted the other functions.

Because the company had grown and spread throughout the universe, the focus was more on solving the numerous day-to-day problems that arose rather than engaging in planning for the success of the business. In some ways, the numerous functions had developed tunnel vision with respect to their individual responsibilities.

One day, the company's founder called you into his spacious office in the stars. He asked you to serve as his chief of staff and to gather your ideas and recommendations on three key issues facing the company:

- Given the growth of the company and emerging functions, what type of planning process would you recommend to help the company stay on track?
- How would you ensure that everyone understood the main mission and objectives of the company, both long- and short-term?
- How would you ensure one integrated plan was created for the new business year?
- What would you recommend?

_____

_____

_____

_____

_____

Manager's Checklist for Chapter 2

☑ Understand the purpose of a business plan.

☑ Use the business plan to identify planning information for next level plans, e.g., functional plans.

☑ Use the planning flow from business plan to key results areas to identify your own KRAs.

☑ Do not plan in a vacuum: Look for opportunities to integrate your plan with interdependencies.

☑ Use the Catchball concept to encourage both vertical and horizontal plan integration.

Measuring Performance

Once the business plan has been created and the next level of planning has occurred from the business plan, performance measurements can be established. Within the hierarchy of planning noted in Chapter 1, the functional and departmental plans will provide more specific input to develop the measurements and performance standards on how to achieve the overall results required in the business plan.

Where we are in this scheme ...

- Strategic Plan ➔ Strategic Objectives (3 Years)
- Annual Business Plan ➔ Mission and Business Objectives
- Functional/Departmental Plan ➔ Mission, Key Results Areas (KRAs) and Specific Objectives
- Individual Performance Plan ➔ Objectives and Measurements

Measurement as Part of a Larger System

Based on a five-year research study I conducted, the following benchmark has been assembled from well-recognized training institutes and companies known for excellence in linking business plans with functional and individual performance plans. The focus of this study was to answer the question, "What's state-of-the-art in managing and measuring performance and productivity?" The responses were consistent from both the training experts and the best-in-class companies. Simply put, all respondents referred to the use of a systematic approach designed to link company strategies, objectives, and measurements to managerial, team, and individual performance at every level. The major idea behind this system is to ensure that effective planning and linkages occur on the front end of the system so that more accurate measurements can be established to guide execution and appraisal of performance on the back end of the system. In most cases, managing performance was used in the same context as managing productivity.

The goal of this benchmark is to provide a model that isn't function or department specific, but is adaptable to several business environments. It's also "forms neutral" and doesn't depend on specific forms, which could easily be created for the function or department.

The Business, Functional, and Individual Performance System outlined in the following presentation integrates the feedback and comments from the survey respondents. This represents the best thinking and execution related to managing performance and productivity.

The Business, Functional, and Individual Performance System

As an integrated system, each component requires detailed planning and completion to effectively link to each other. The biggest problems consistent with failure to execute this system are disconnects among the integration of these components. When steps are missed or incomplete it will make all the downstream planning less effective. What follows is a detailed explanation of each component in this system flow in Exhibit 3-1.

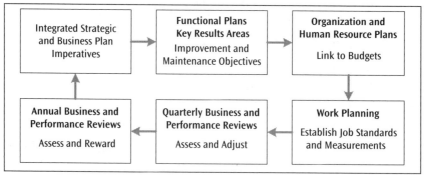

Exhibit 3-1. Planning system flow

Company Strategies and Annual Business Plan Imperatives

The goal of this component is to provide a link from the overall company direction to the specific functions and departments. This information serves two purposes: (1) provides a top-level view of the strategies, priorities, and macro measurements, and (2) allows for the alignment of the organization in more detailed plans for functional objectives and individual and team performance planning. The goal of this effort would be to have every individual in the organization quickly see how their work is linked to the overall business performance.

Functional Plans and Objectives

Each function should take this information and determine how it specifically relates to the direction and objectives of the departments and units delivering work products and services. It's important to identify user requirements. Once these objectives are determined, the functional leaders can focus on identifying the required structure and processes needed to achieve the results. Once you've completed this work, a human resource plan can be developed that identifies the skills, competencies, and staffing levels required to achieve the results. The final link is the annual operating budget in terms of fixed annual expenses. The rollup of this information allows the financial group to complete the company budget.

Categories of Objectives

Maintenance. Maintenance objectives (also called operational objectives) are the day-to-day requirements for running a business function.

Improvement. Improvement objectives are written each year to implement a process, program, or initiative to improve the operation of the function and delivery of services to both internal and external customers.

Other Initiatives. Initiatives will take the form of specific projects that may be cross-functional and will lead to achieving larger-scale, breakthrough progress toward company strategic objectives.

SMART Criteria for Writing Objectives

The acronym may be overused, but it bears reference here as a standard to measure well-written objectives. This is the test that objectives must pass to be effective:

Specific. Stated in precise, not vague terms. Objectives are quantified.

Measurable. Measurements are included to provide targets for the objectives.

Attainable. Objectives are realistic but challenging and provide "stretch" to be attained.

Relevant. Objectives must link to the business and functional objectives.

Timely. Dates for completion are included in the objectives.

Preparing the Functional Plan

In terms of preparing the functional plan, let's assume that you've identified your mission and key results areas and then drafted a set of functional objectives. Although this work may be considered preliminary, it will provide the backdrop to completing the next steps in the plan. The list in the following sidebar of planning principles can be used as a guide.

THE PLAN PREPARATION FLOW

FOR EXAMPLE

Mission

Part 1. Key Result Areas
- Derived from the Business Plan
✔ Completed

Part 2. Objectives
- Maintenance
- Improvement
- Other

Part 3. Organization and Human Resource Plans
- Link to Annual Budgets

Part 4. Performance Standards and Measurements Established

Part 5. How Tracked

A completed sample plan is available on pages 49–50.

Organization and Human Resource Planning

On completion of the mission, key results areas, and functional objectives, the next phase is to complete the organization and human resource plans that will provide the final input for the budget. There's a tendency to jump from objective setting to budget projects, using the current organization framework. It's critical that the organization structure and processes be reviewed every year to then determine the skill and staffing requirements. This can be considered a strategic activity because the output will match the human assets requirements to the needs of the organization for any given year. This will have a significant impact on the fixed annual budget, so it shouldn't be taken lightly. The process to be undertaken flows essentially like this:

In organization planning, use the specified key results areas and major objectives to determine the requirements for the future organization necessary to "deliver the function" or achieve the expected results. The goal is to have the right structure in place with the right functionality to do this.

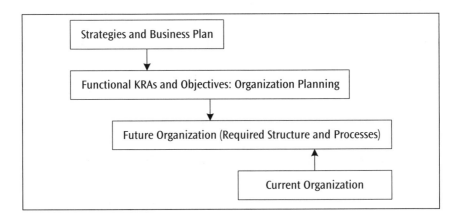

Planning Principles

- Structure should facilitate the execution of strategy and objectives.
- Structural design and core process identification will lead to human resource requirements. Form follows function and that determines the people side.
- Flatter structures are desirable because they increase the speed of decision making and enhance the visibility of the function.

- Processes should be designed with as few handoffs as possible because they tend to be obstacles to process speed.
- There's no one perfect structure. One common denominator is how to best serve the customer.

Critical success factors such as degree of specialization, responding to a dynamic environment, team-based versus individual-focused work, managing projects (scope and size factors), and mode of operation for growth, stability, or consolidation must be considered in creating the best structure. With this in mind, use the following procedure to complete the structure and process design.

Begin with a layout of the current organization. Identify the sub-functions needed to meet the functional objectives and priorities for the coming business year. List the subfunctions that must be added to the current scheme. Identify those subfunctions that may be combined or eliminated because they're not mission-critical and/or don't add value for the customer. The subfunctions can be arranged in a way to keep the design as flat as possible yet accommodate the design principles and critical success factors expressed earlier. For each of the subfunctions, create bullet points for the competencies required for successful execution. Once this preliminary design has been conceptualized, it should be framed as the link to the next step: business process evaluation. List the core subprocesses managed within the function. Review their effectiveness regarding how well they support the execution of the company strategy and functional objectives. A formal procedure may be employed at this point, including business process improvement, value stream mapping, or another relevant technique. The last step is to create an organization chart for the required organization structure.

This will feed the next downstream planning activity.

Human Resource Planning

The next step is to integrate human resource planning with organization planning to determine the skills required to deliver the results. This will require a review of the competencies needed for success that will be compared to current skill sets in the current organization. This analysis will produce a gap analysis and will feed the hiring, training, and development of people to fill voids identified, which is basically the staffing plan going into the business year. In the staffing plan you'll want to identify the total number of full-time employees (FTE), which includes supervision levels. You should plan three approaches to the staffing plan: staffing at 100% of revenue, staffing at 75% of revenue, and staffing at 125% of revenue. This will help to plan for contingencies during the business year as they arise. The flow will look like this:

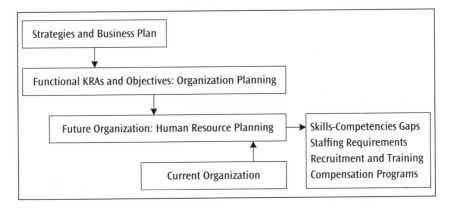

The sample staffing plan—headcount on page 46 indicates that one new professional buyer will be added. In addition, the competencies of the buyers will require specialization in new technical supplies to support product development. An external hire is indicated with training for existing personnel.

ORGANIZATION AND HUMAN RESOURCE PLANNING

FOR EXAMPLE

Purchasing Department

Mission Statement (state the purpose of the function and what it provides to the business)

Typical Subfunctions
- Materials management
- Inventory management

Typical Core Subprocesses
- Procurement
- Supplier relations and contracts
- Inventory control

Staffing Plan—Headcount

Level	Current	Projected
MANAGEMENT		
Manager of Purchasing	1	1
Supervisor of Purchasing	1	1
PROFESSIONAL		
Buyers	3	4
Material Controller	1	1
Clerical and Administrative	3	3

Organization planning and design This is a process that enables the creation of the wiring diagram that will identify the required functions and processes to drive business strategies

KEY TERM and functional objectives to a successful conclusion. In addition, clear lines of authority and accountability must be established to create the reporting controls needed for effective management. The structure should be designed to increase the speed of information flow and decision making and eliminate bureaucracy. The new norm is the flatter organization.

Work Planning and Individual Performance Standards

In this component each department, through the department manager, meets with every employee to link their work (to the extent possible) to the overall company objectives and user requirements. They establish expectations along with standards of performance to serve as the guide to performance and productivity measurement.

Major Objectives-Setting Errors

There are many reasons why functional objectives fail to be achieved. Here are 10 reasons objectives fail.

1. Objectives are set too high or too low and, therefore, are demotivating.
2. Objectives are dictated, not negotiated to the extent possible.
3. Objectives are not tied to strategic or business objectives.
4. Objectives are not tied to individual and team performance standards.

5. Objectives are not communicated to external interdependencies.
6. Objectives lack flexibility, especially in light of dynamic business conditions.
7. Objectives are not tracked or reviewed periodically.
8. Objectives conflict with leader and subordinates.
9. Achievement of objectives goes unrewarded.
10. There is a lack of consequences for unmet objectives.

PERSISTENCE SMART

Persistence or "stick-to-it-iveness" means that objectives are set to demand the best of each person. In addition, this MANAGING effort must be accompanied by a strong desire or passion to make it happen. Challenging objectives must be monitored and reviewed periodically for progress against the plan results. Be a tough critic of your own progress and surround yourself with encouraging people who can provide honest feedback. Don't blame others if you fall short; you're looking for a lesson to learn in every situation.

Developing Individual Performance Standards from the Functional Mission, Key Results, and Objectives

Performance Analysis. Performance analysis is the process of gathering information about the content of a specific job, which will become the basis for planning, job performance, productivity, and appraisal. Every individual should have a job specification that guides them in successfully performing the job.

Considerations. Look at the tasks, projects, job functions, and output of the work being performed. Link these specific tasks, projects, and job functions to quantitative and qualitative measures that will help achieve the functional key results/objectives and contribute to the overall mission. This will form the basis of what's evaluated in performance appraisal (quantity, quality, timeliness, cost, and customer satisfaction).

Identify Skills Necessary to Reach Successful Performance. Identify job behaviors needed for successful performance, including key areas such as interpersonal relations, communications, and time management.

Performance Standards. Setting clear performance standards facilitates successful operations in the following ways:

- Provide mutually agreed-on direction for employee efforts.
- Linked to broader strategic imperatives, departmental objectives, and user requirements.
- Facilitate self-evaluation and sense of achievement.
- Focus attention on results/outcomes.
- Provide a basis for performance evaluation.
- Support a "pay for performance" philosophy.
- Create a vehicle for identifying skill development opportunities.

Writing Performance Standards and Measurements

A well-written performance standard will be integrated with the functional priorities and is a description of what will be accomplished and how the results of the actions taken will be measured. Again, it should meet the SMART criteria mentioned earlier in the chapter.

Here are some examples of effective performance standards:

- Reduce call waiting time by 25% this quarter, decreasing from the current rate of 2 minutes to 1.5 minutes, as tracked by the telephone audit logs.
- Complete Sales Optimization Process for our customer base by end of quarter 2, measured by the completion and assignment of resources in Sales Optimization Matrix.
- Increase on-time deliveries from 95% to 98% by the end of quarter 4 as measured by the year-end order fulfillment report.

The following list identifies some typical quantitative measurements.

Output Quantity
- Number of sales
- Items entered in a ledger
- Number of documents completed
- Earnings on commissions
- Number of calls per day
- Reports completed by [date]

Quality
- Cost of rejected work
- Items entered in a ledger
- Errors
- Number of returned goods
- Warranty costs
- Percent of positive customer satisfaction

Safety
- Lost time accidents

Sales Volume (Output)
- Penetration of the market (share)

Controlling Expenses
- Reduction in expenses from previous period
- Number and value of new cost-reducing procedures

Profit Realization
- Return on net assets
- Percentage of profits to sales
- Gross profit by product line

Technical Accomplishments
- Completed on time and within budget
- Cost of each research project against budget
- Extent of contribution and amount of innovation in the project (i.e., highly creative ideas)
- Dollars of savings realized from projects

Sample Functional Plan

The following illustrates a sample functional plan for purchasing and the assurance of supplier quality.

Purchasing: Supplier Quality Assurance

Mission
Manage partnerships with world-class suppliers who are committed to the objectives of innovation, quick response, best total cost, and continuous improvement.

Part 1. Key Results Areas
- Supplier cost and quality management
- Increase customer satisfaction
- Contribute to company profitability objectives
- ✔ Completed

Part 2. Objectives
- Maintenance
- Complete monthly supplier audits
- Optimize material purchases—meet schedules
- Improvement
- Improve use of information technology in managing the function
- Increase the number of suppliers involved in stage one of the new product development process

- Other: Increase skill levels of employees with respect to Lean Techniques and other productivity tools

Part 3. Organization and Human Resource Plans
- Future organization structure and processes needed to achieve the mission and objectives
- Human assets required to do the job and the cost of labor and expenses
- Link to annual budgets

Part 4. Performance Standards and Measurements Established
- Each individual has a performance plan linked to the function, with measurements

Part 5. How Tracked
- Use the tools and techniques outlined in the planning toolkit in the Appendix.

Tracking the Objectives

The ability to both track and influence the success of the objectives will be improved by using the tools and techniques outlined in the Appendix to this book. For example, tools such as Pareto, cause-and-effect diagrams, and check sheets will assist in both determining the baseline measurements and tracking the progress of the objectives, especially where aggressive improvement targets have been set. The tracking column can be completed by selecting specific tools from the toolkit. The tracking of the objectives is not limited to only those tools mentioned in this book.

Review of Progress

The most effective method of determining performance to plan is to conduct quarterly business reviews that are combined with feedback to employees regarding how they're performing versus the standards of performance established in the work planning phase. The goal of quarterly reviews is to assess the degree to which things are going according to plan. This allows adjustments to be made and contingency plans to be activated if needed. In addition, annual reviews look back on the past business year and evaluate the employee performance against the established standards of performance. The business performance review will determine how well the company met its commitments to stakeholders and may provide the basis for additional rewards such as bonuses. Employees will be evaluated on the degree of completion and contribution in terms of a rating and salary increase. In-depth information will be provided in Chapter 7.

Creating the Right Mindset Regarding Measurement

Here's a way to think about changing the mindset toward aggressive measurement of customer requirements:

Old Ways	Right Mindset
▪ Added Work ▪ A Cookbook Solution ▪ Measure Mania ▪ The Quality Department's Responsibility	▪ A Method of Prioritizing Work ▪ A Discipline of Action ▪ A System to Define Expectations and Deliver on Them ▪ Everyone's Responsibility

IMPACT VERSUS ACTIVITY

CAUTION

The warning signal is that you may not be focusing on the right priorities. The danger here is to focus more on the activity versus the impact of that activity on the business. One way to create the right focus is to think about eliminating non-value-added activities—the activities that don't add value for the customer. Find ways to reduce paperwork through electronic communications. Look for redundant or duplicative activities and streamline them.

Converting Customer Requirements into Measurements

As a working example, the goal of this project is to establish key performance measures and to develop supporting programs to improve customer service and satisfaction levels. The results of this effort will directly impact the strategic and business plan objectives regarding increases in market share, customer retention, and operating income. The end results will also help to create and maintain a competitive advantage in the marketplace.

The process of converting the voice of the customer (VOC) into deployable measurements is outlined below and will be illustrated with a concrete example that will serve as a baseline for creating other measurements.

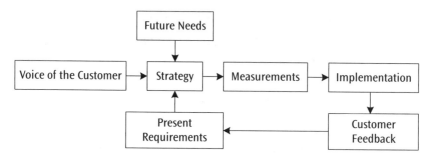

How the VOC Process Will Produce Improvements

The process will ensure that your products and services consistently meet and exceed the customer requirements if it's implemented in the following manner.

Obtain feedback from the customer to gain valuable input on present requirements and future needs. This should be accomplished by short, concise surveys done either online or via mail. In certain situations, face-to-face focus groups may be more advantageous.

Analyze the feedback, and based on the requirements that customers rate as important, review your current measurements to see if there's a match for the requirement. For example, the question of responsiveness of the company representatives to resolve issues receives high importance ratings. If you don't have an accurate method of measuring this,

---

CONVERSION TABLE

- Customer Requirement: Responsiveness
- Attributes: Order fill rate, cycle time, on-time delivery
- Performance Standard: 100% of fill rate, five days turnaround, within two hours
- Measurements: Actual versus goals in percent achieved
- Process: Flowchart all activities that impact performance and identify process improvements, e.g., forecast accuracy, sales input accuracy, inventory planning, etc.

TOOLS

you'll want to create a more precise measurement. An example of this conversion is shown in the table on page 52.

Linking Planning and Budgets

The last step in completing the functional plan is to prepare the annual budget estimate for review and approval by the finance team. This will ensure that the company total budget will meet the revenue and profitability targets specified in the business plan.

Bringing the Planning Data Forward

The annual budget estimate will be composed of the total expenses required to meet the functional mission, key results areas, and major objectives (maintenance, improvement, and other). The expenses will include labor and administrative costs.

Labor Expenses	Base Salary	Benefits
Management	_____	_____
Salaried	_____	_____
Hourly	_____	_____
Subtotals		
Total Labor		
Operating Expenses	Amount	
Supplies and Equipment (non-capital)	_____	
Outside Services	_____	
Other Expenses	_____	
Total Expenses		
Total Annual Expenses		

Aligning Priorities

One of the most important skills of managers working in a resource-lean environment is to be able to align priorities to ensure they're working on the right priorities at any given time. It's inevitable that unplanned

---

NEW ROLE OF THE FUNCTIONAL MANAGER

FOR EXAMPLE

The role of the traditional functional manager has shifted from the basic responsibilities of scheduling and controlling to one of leadership. In this new role, the functional manager is responsible for hiring the right people and creating a work climate in which employees *want* to produce results, not *have to*. The new role involves the ability to remove obstacles that block productivity and develop employees so they continuously learn new techniques to apply to day-to-day problem solving.

---

priorities will come up, so the challenge is how to sort out what's most important to the business and customers.

Three skills are directly linked to success in this area:

Priority Setting. These individuals are able to quickly zero in on the mission-critical priorities by assessing where the lower-value priorities really are. They can eliminate roadblocks that hurt productivity and can sense what's helping or hindering progress immediately. They spend time thinking about these priorities every day.

Action-Oriented. These individuals create energy and action for everyone they work with. They can take calculated risks and have a high success rate. They are comfortable with their actions and rarely reverse direction.

Timely Decision Making. These individuals are able to make swift, unbiased decisions and meet or exceed deadlines in every situation under their control. They can act within all information others may need to initiative decisive actions.

Exercise: Your Inbox

You have just returned to the office after a week of much needed vacation time. You know that the first day back will be critical to assess priorities and make sure the department is on track to meet its objectives for the quarter. As you look up you see the poster on the wall with the key business priorities for the year: Business Growth, Take Time for People, Productivity, and Financial Management.

As you scan your inbox, the following issues arise (not in priority order). Your task is to prioritize these issues and begin to take the required action. You should think about what is most urgent and important to the business as you sort things out.

1. You have received a resignation from one of your key employees. It seems he is going to a competitor and you have concerns about conflicts of interest.

2. A marketing manager has left you an urgent message that you need to participate in a conference call regarding pricing issues. You're aware of the problem.

3. You've been asked to evaluate a new software package that's critical to your department's productivity.

4. One of your delivery trucks has broken down, creating havoc in the daily schedule.

5. You were notified by the credit department that a large electronic cash transfer from one of your biggest customers did not occur as planned.

6. A local university has asked you to make a short presentation this week to an engineering class. You had to cancel prior to vacation and this is one of the best intern and recruitment sources for your company.

7. You are informed that two employees didn't show up for work today because of severe weather in the area. You are already short-handed in that work area.

What will you do? What actions will you take immediately? How will you adjust the priorities around these issues to focus on the right things?

_____

_____

_____

_____

_____

_____

_____

_____

Of course, there are no prescribed answers. The key to success is to determine what actions come first. This may be accomplished in a number of ways, including delegation and timely communications.

CONFLICTING PRIORITIES

CAUTION A project manager was given four projects from key customers at the same time. All were deemed high-priority, and they were due at approximately the same time. Two of the projects would involve further review to clarify requirements. This, of course, was on top of existing commitments. The concern was how to satisfy all customers. In this situation, the project manager went to his immediate manager to ask for a "judgment call," in which the priorities were adjusted according to the urgency of the individual customers to meet their business goals. Matching the priority with the urgency need helped to sort out what got done. It may be difficult to sort out at times, but is an excellent starting point to resolve conflicts of this type.

Manager's Checklist for Chapter 3

☑ Understand measurement as part of the overall planning system.

☑ Understand the components of a functional plan.

☑ Use the flowcharts for organization and human resource planning.

☑ Use the guidelines for preparing performance standards and measurements.

☑ Link plans and budgets.

☑ Create the right mindset to be an effective planner.

☑ Assess your ability to align priorities.

Execution Is
the Key

O ne way to look at execution is as part of a strategic process in which execution, implementation, or deployment is the end product. The overall process is called *strategic management.* In this planning and management process, it can be considered a hierarchy of ideas that emanates from the top but is interactive to reach its final state.

Strategic thinking is the process used by leaders to create a vision for the future.

Strategic planning and strategy formulation is the process used to develop supporting analyses (external environment, competitive, SWOT, etc.), communicate and implement a chosen strategy, and answer the questions: "Where are we now?" "Where do we go?" "How do we get there?"

Strategy deployment is the process designed to drive strategy and business plans throughout the organization so that the overall priorities of the company are aligned from top to bottom. Much of the input gathered in strategic planning is downloaded into increments of normally three years and lands in some type of organization framework. Often the business plan serves as the first step in arriving at this framework.

The framework is used to create visibility for what is important to focus on and to achieve as a business. The tools reviewed in this chapter

SMART MANAGING

STRIVING FOR EXCELLENCE

Proactive managers recognize that when people try new ideas and approaches, they don't succeed every time. The goal is not to encourage mistakes but to be aware that they will occur. Part of the motivation for having long-term objectives is that you have opportunities to handle problems and make adjustments along the way. One excellent reading resource is *Failing Forward* by John C. Maxwell, in which he demonstrates the power of learning from mistakes. This can be a difficult task for some managers who try to forget mistakes rather than learn from them. Once you master the ability to learn from mistakes, the opportunities for continuous improvement are endless.

outline several methods of supporting strategy deployment, often referred to as *policy deployment*. It may be positioned prior to, during, or after functional plans have been drafted. The most important factor in the success of this alignment process is that it is interactive until finalized.

The first step in preparing for execution of strategies and business plans is to evaluate your readiness for successful execution. The Malcolm Baldrige Systems Perspective is an excellent way to assess your readiness and identify gaps. This should be done prior to the final selection of the deployment tool and mobilization of the workforce.

Malcolm Baldrige Systems Perspective

The Malcolm Baldrige Quality Award Program was created in 1987 and is supported by the Malcolm Baldridge Quality Award Foundation. Although its main purpose is to foster the improvement of quality, costs, and productivity, the systems perspective looks at the key components necessary to run a successful business.

Many companies have used the Malcolm Baldrige criteria as a method of building excellence in organization performance. Awards are given to companies that meet these criteria and produce outstanding business results. The perspective can provide a systematic method of approaching strategy deployment by making sure that the building blocks for successful performance are in place. This model can serve as both a planning and auditing tool.

Baldrige Criteria for Performance Excellence Framework

The Baldrige categories can be visualized as shown in Exhibit 4-1.

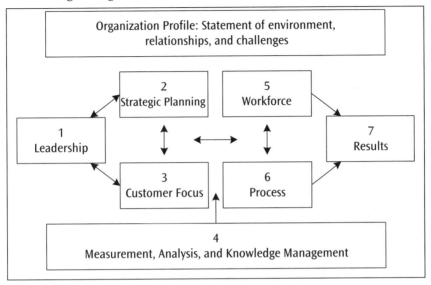

Exhibit 4-1. Baldrige categories

Using the Baldrige Framework

For each of the seven categories create a strategy and supporting objectives that can be used for planning, auditing, and deployment purposes. In the Baldridge System, points are given for the degree to which an organization meets the criteria in each category.

This framework is, presented as an initial approach to assessing the organization rather than scoring the components outlined in the systems perspective. After answering the questions in each category, you will find a summary table (Exhibit 4-2) to capture strengths, weaknesses, and gaps to fill. This will be a strong aid into successful deployment.

1. Leadership (Ability of senior leaders to guide and sustain the company for long-term success)

Focus areas for execution:

■ How well do senior leaders create a focus on action to accomplish their objectives, improve performance, and attain the company's vision?

■ How well do senior leaders include a focus on setting overall objectives and expectations?

2. Strategic Planning (Ability to develop a strategic plan that's deployable)

Focus areas for execution:

■ Does the company have effective strategic and business planning processes?

■ What are the key strategic objectives, strategies, plans, and timetable for accomplishing them?

■ To what extent are action plans in place to ensure the plans are achieved?

3. Customer Focus (Ability to use customer and market knowledge)

Focus areas for execution:

■ How well do you identify customers, customer groups, and market segments?

■ How well do you define the target customers, customer groups, and market segments to pursue for current and future products and services?

■ How well do you analyze customer satisfaction, dissatisfaction, and loyalty?

4. Measurement, Analysis, and Knowledge Management (Ability to measure, analyze, align, review, and improve performance data and information at all levels and in all parts of the organization)

Focus areas for execution:

■ How well do you select, collect, align, and integrate data and information for tracking daily operations and for tracking overall organizational performance? This includes progress relative to strategic objectives and action plans.

■ How well established are your key organizational performance measures?

■ How effectively do you use these data and information to support organizational decision making?

5. Workforce Focus (Ability to enable employees to accomplish the work of the organization)

Focus areas for execution:

■ How does your employee performance management system, including feedback to employees, support high-performance work and contribute to the achievement of your action plans?

■ How well does your employee performance management system support a customer and business focus?

■ How well do your compensation, recognition, and related reward and incentive practices reinforce a high-performance work climate and a customer focus?

6. Process Management (Ability to identify and manage key processes)

Focus areas for execution:

■ How well do you design these processes to meet all the key requirements?

■ How well do you incorporate new technology, organizational knowledge, and the potential need for agility into the design of these processes?

■ How well do you incorporate cycle time, productivity, cost control, and other efficiency and effectiveness factors into the design of these processes? How do you implement these processes to ensure they meet design requirements?

7. Results (Ability to achieve expected results)

Focus areas for execution:

■ How well are you able to determine the final results as they're measured against the business plan commitments?

LEADING WITH VISION

The dialogue from *Alice in Wonderland* illustrates the importance of vision. As Alice confronts the Cheshire Cat, she asks, "Would you tell me, please, which way I ought to go from here?" "That depends a good deal on where you want to get to," replies the cat. With the vision expressed as a place you want to reach at a future point in time, it becomes easier to identify the pathways to get there. The organization expects its leaders to share a vision of the future because knowing the company has a clear direction is motivating and gives a sense of security to the organization.

System Perspective Area	Strengths (What is the organization doing well?)	Weaknesses (What is the organization doing poorly?)	Gaps to Fill (What must be improved imme-diately to support effective execution?)
Leadership			
Strategic Planning			
Customer Focus			
Measurement			
Workforce			
Process Management			
Results			

Exhibit 4-2. Summary table for Baldrige execution planning

Balanced Scorecard

Introduced in 1992 *The Balanced Scorecard* was written by Robert Kaplan and David Norton and is regarded as the most commonly used framework for ensuring that companies can execute their strategies. Today, about 70% of the Fortune 1,000 companies use an approach that employs either the Balanced Scorecard or some other vehicle to help manage performance. The scorecard format contains a central list of metrics/measurements, as explained below, which are drivers of the organization's success. These categories include areas such as financials, people, operations, suppliers, customers, and support systems. The numbers should measure not just important outcomes, but also the focus areas that influence or drive those outcomes.

Balanced Scorecard Model

Vision Statement. The vision statement is set in the center of a balanced scorecard as a way to create a unified view of the future. It should be a compelling statement of what the company is striving to be and do in the marketplace at a future point in time that everyone in the company can relate to.

Focus areas for the vision statement. Coupled with the vision statement, these are the focus areas for the company. These focus areas can be considered the high-level drivers of the business. The classic categories include:

- **Financial Perspective**: How does the company look to its stakeholders?
  - Strategies: Grow revenues by 15%
  - Metric/Measurement: Revenue and gross margin targets/actual versus targets
- **Customer Perspective**: How does the company look to its customers?
  - Strategies: Increase customer retention and satisfaction rates
  - Metric/Measurement: Customer retention/turnover rate
- **Internal Business Processes Perspective**: What business processes must the company excel at?
  - Strategies: Improve the new product development and selling processes
  - Metric/Measurement: Core processes listed/percent of reengineered processes
- **People and Learning Perspective**: How can the company improve its net talent value?
  - Strategies: Become the employer of choice
  - Metric/Measurement: Retain best talent/involuntary turnover rates

Other Categories for Consideration:
- **Growth and Innovation:** New product/service introductions
  - Strategies: Introduce specific products/services ahead of the competition
  - Metric/Measurement: Actual versus planned
- **Core Capabilities:** Unique capabilities to strengthen
  - Strategies: Identify specific capabilities to focus on, e.g., product marketing
  - Metric/Measurement: Number of new customers

Populating the Balanced Scorecard Model

Using the templates below, the Balanced Scorecard can be created using the strategies and metrics/measurements identified. These are examples and should limit the use of other relevant information.

Two templates are presented to import your planning information. Template #1 focuses on the four most common elements found in a Balanced Scorecard. As this template is completed, it will feed the next level of plans, typically for functions and departments. In template #2 there is some variation in the focus areas, as well as a more detailed look at critical success factors and measurement. This approach provides more direction to the next level of plans and allows for customization as it cascades through the organization. The notion here is that each function could have a Balanced Scorecard that ties into the overall company plan. Exhibits 4-3 and 4-4 illustrate templates for creating and executing a Balanced Scorecard.

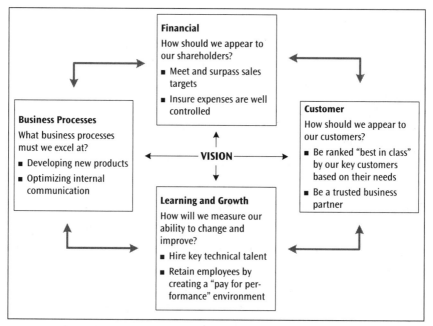

Exhibit 4-3. Template #1: Developing a Balanced Scorecard

A Balanced Scorecard can be used as a way to organize the strategic and business objectives and provide input into the further development of a functional plan. The finalization of functional plans is an iterative process, with the alignment to company objectives being a major factor in determining the key results and supporting objectives.

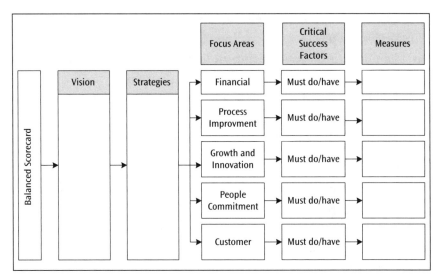

Exhibit 4-4. Template #2: Developing a balanced scorecard

Hoshin Planning

Hoshin Planning originated in Japan at the Kobe Shipyards in the mid-1960s. *Hoshin Kanri* means setting a direction similar to that of a ship's compass that aids the ship and its crew to reach their destination. This is done in tandem with the monitoring and control of the voyage. The Hoshin System is designed as a complete planning and deployment process that has some similarity to the MBO process developed in the mid-1970s in the United States. It's a systematic planning methodology that defines a long-range objective without losing focus on the day-to-day measurements required to run the business. This is an effective way to ensure that the entire organization is working toward the same objectives—without regard to the level function, department, or individual. In some applications, an annual breakthrough objective is identified and the organization makes subsequent plans to achieve it. The breakthrough objective may be called "vision" in other deployment tools.

Attributes of Hoshin Planning

■ Aligns the organization on achieving the strategic objectives.

■ Ensures that everyone is heading in the same direction with a sense of control.

- Assists employees to understand the long-range direction and makes the vision a reality.
- Identifies critical issues facing the organization (i.e., profitability, cost savings).
- Facilitates breakthrough activities to help achieve significant performance improvement.
- Emphasizes real-time corrective actions for continuous improvement.

Hoshin Planning Table

The Hoshin Planning Table may be configured in a number of ways, depending on the information desired. The example presented in Exhibit 4-5 is designed to bring forward the key information from strategic and business planning, which can be used to align various company functions to it.

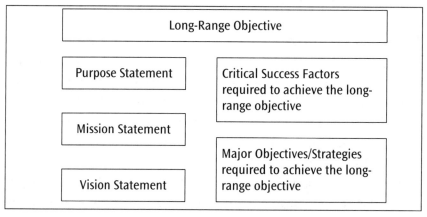

Exhibit 4-5. Hoshin Planning Table for aligning strategy and function

Driving Forces Wheel

The Driving Forces Wheel was used by Black and Decker North American Power Tools in the mid-1990s as a vehicle to focus attention on the key drivers of the business and to rally all company managers to communicate with their employees about the direction of the company and engage them in more detailed planning around each of the driving forces (Exhibit 4-6).

A short description of each position on the wheel is provided to clarify the meaning and importance of each of the driving forces so that a standardized message is presented and provides a way to align the organization.

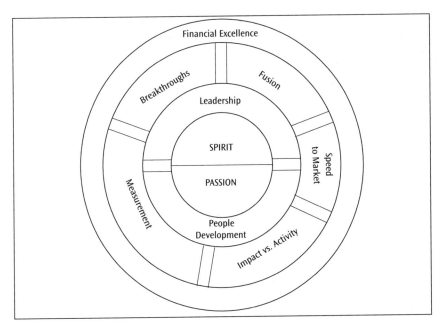

Exhibit 4-6. Driving Forces Wheel

Financial Excellence. Focus on the key indicators of operating income, market share, RONA, etc. Every unit manager must understand the profit and loss statement and its impact on the financials, such as cash flow. A major emphasis is on moving from top-line sales growth to overall financial performance.

Fusion. Focus on creating the seamless organization. Break down silos (isolation) and improve communications across functions and departments that are interdependent and must work together for the company's success. Increase the speed and quality of decision making and use cross-functional product development as a way to drive new products to the market.

Speed to Market. Focus on learning faster than the competition; rapid learning is critical to the success of the company and will give a competitive advantage over time. One example of the application is to integrate customer requirements with new technology. The goal is to build speed into everything the company does, and this affects all functions and departments.

Breakthroughs. Focus on breakthrough thinking by breaking existing paradigms. Think beyond incremental improvements and look for quantum leaps in progress, e.g., reducing cycle times by greater than 40%. Be creative and innovative with new products.

Measurement. Focus on measuring the right things. Things that get measured will become priorities. This will be the key to continuous improvement and total quality management for the company. Focus on the key measurements of cost, quality, and speed—all must be balanced to create an advantage over the competition.

FOR EXAMPLE

BREAKING PARADIGMS

Integrating the measurements of cost, quality, and speed requires shifting paradigms to create competitive advantage. The new paradigms are that shorter cycle times reduce resource cost (not increase it) and high quality can be achieved with shorter cycle times (not longer ones). This new thinking erases the old way of thinking often characterized by the saying, "Cost, quality, and speed—pick any two." One of the best examples of making this new paradigm work is Toyota Motor Company. Its motto for its high-end Lexus, "The Relentless Pursuit of Perfection," epitomizes this and demonstrates the integration of this thinking in the production processes.

Impact vs. Activity. Focus on the right priorities; eliminate non-value-added work. Reduce paperwork, only reporting on necessary and required information. Keep your focus on actions that keep the business moving forward. Take actions with high impact and return on the investment of time and money. Think, "What's the best use of my time and skills right now?"

Leadership. Focus on your ability to influence others to produce positive results. Create energy in your interactions with others. Share your vision of the future and engage people around their responsibility to drive the company forward and share in its success.

People Development. Focus on skill development. Ensure that every employee feels they possess the skills to do their jobs at a high level. Provide training and development support as an ongoing process in every department.

Spirit and Passion. Focus on the intangibles, which stir excitement and enthusiasm in others. It's the "fire in the belly" and the neverending quest to be a recognized industry leader in everything we do.

> **MANAGEMENT BY WALKING AROUND**
>
> *TRICKS OF THE TRADE*
>
> Management visibility is an inherent quality in the engagement of others. Many managers are criticized by their employees because they're inaccessible. This has been more of a factor in organizations that have downsized. In these situations managers have taken on more of a hands-on workload and have less time to interact with their people. This cannot be used as an excuse, however, even though it's a major challenge in time management. Whether a company is capital- or labor-intensive, it's still about people focusing on the right things.

Strategy Deployment Worksheet

The Strategy Deployment Worksheet is an alignment tool designed as an aid to functional planning. It's a method of tracking key result areas and objectives against the overall business plan and strategies. It serves as an excellent tool to eliminate gaps in the planning process. Because the worksheet is best used as a link to the next level of planning, it is described in detail in Chapter 5 as a tool to help mobilize the workforce.

Other Deployment Tools

Almost every process can be viewed as a closed system in which there are three buckets: inputs, a process of action, and outputs that deliver a final product. This idea lends itself well to creating a planning tool and mental model for any manager to use in either high-level or tactical planning. In its most practical format, you gather information in each of the three buckets and then convert it into specific measurements for use in detailed phases.

McKinsey 7 S Model

The McKinsey 7 S Framework (Strategy, Shared Values, Structure, Systems, Style, Staffing, and Skills) was developed by Tom Peters and Robert Waterman to focus attention on the seven factors that must be carefully aligned so an organization can excel, produce products and services of high quality, satisfy its customers, fulfill its employees, and make a profit. This model can create a strategy and business plan, identify priorities, and set direction for the future. The process of applying the 7 S model may be divided into three distinct phases with the goal of using the information gathered for both planning and alignment purposes.

- Phase 1: Setting the direction, business strategy, core capabilities, and shared values
- Phase 2: Organization Planning—Establishing requirements for the future organization and identifying the gap between that and today's organization
- Phase 3: Strategic Human Resources—Applying strategic human resource techniques to close the gaps

The box below illustrates how to use this model in the three phases of this process.

PHASE 1: SETTING DIRECTION, BUSINESS STRATEGY, AND SHARED VALUES

Phase 1.

S Factor 1. Strategy and Core Capabilities (What is the direction and business strategy going forward, and what are the core capabilities?)

Examples:

Strategies
- Manage profitable growth (10–15%)
- Identify, create, and open new markets
- Leverage current products and services

Core Capabilities
- Superior technology and products
- Operational excellence
- Engaged and talented workforce

S Factor 2. Shared Values (What are the values that will distinguish the organization in the marketplace?)

Examples:
- Focus on and dedication to the customer
- Demonstrate ethical behavior
- Embrace change

Phase 2: How Will You Build the Future Organization?

S Factor 3. Structure (How should you be structured to deliver the results?)

Examples:
- Flat, focused decisions and team-based

S Factor 4. Systems (What systems and processes will be required to deliver the results?)

Examples:
- Communication and information systems

S Factor 5. Style (What are the executive and management competencies required to deliver the results?)

Examples:
- Create vision and purpose
- Mobilize people and resources
- Critical thinking
- Manage relationships

Phase 3: Getting the People Right

S Factor 6. Skills (What skill sets will be required to deliver the results?)

Examples:
- Self-reliant problem-solving
- Critical thinking
- Interpersonal savvy

S Factor 7. Staffing (How do you ensure the talent is available to deliver the results?)
- Succession planning and talent reviews and staffing strategy

Business Initiative Planning and Execution

Business Initiative Planning and Execution identifies opportunities and risks of initiatives critical to the success of the company. Business initiatives can come from the strategic plan or business plan and are usually company-wide projects that cross functional lines. The initiatives are assigned an executive sponsor and champion to ensure that the projects are supported during the execution stage. Prior to launching these initiatives, a plan is prepared and approved by the executive leaders. A typical business initiative plan includes:

- Defined goals and benchmarks.
- Recommended actions.
- Justification for recommended actions with appropriate information (market research, qualitative and quantitative opportunities, etc.).
- Identification of key action items, timing of these action items, and who will have responsibility for their execution.
- Communication to other stakeholders as appropriate such as customers, suppliers, sales force, etc.

Business initiatives may fall into areas such as technology implementation and may focus on key areas such as enterprise networks, new product development, and supply chain management. The common elements of the deliverables include:

- Clear definition of opportunity (What, When, Who, Why)
- Objectives and goals (SMART)
- Risk assessment
- Summary of alternatives
- Strategic impact
- Financial impact
- Legal considerations, when appropriate

Sample Business Initiative Recommendation: Use the completed sample template in Exhibit 4-7 to guide your business initiative planning and execution.

Initiative	Private Label Computers—Product Development: The Portable Image Computer
Sponsor Champion	Executive Vice President—Sales and Marketing Vice President—Marketing
Executive Summary	Private Label Computers has an excellent opportunity to leverage its office computer brand, with the use of new technology with existing technology to expand capabilities of current office systems. The Portable Image Computer has the potential to elevate the brand and both create and take market share from our competitors. We will be able to utilize existing marketing programs and channels, including existing customer base, to sell the new product.
Situation	Sales for our "bread and butter" products are off sharply. New competitors enter this field every year. New competition is not coming from other manufacturers of office systems, although this arena remains viable. Rather, the new competition is from a host of new personal computer products that offer additional software programs and capabilities, including many imaging applications. The majority of these products are standalone and do not integrate with other systems.

Exhibit 4-7. Sample template to guide planning and execution (continued on next page)

Situation (continued)	These products appear to create competition at the low end of our business, but the wide growing popularity has the potential for double-digit growth during the next 3–5 years.
Alternatives	Create a standalone product that competes directly with the competitive products, adding features that are more desirable to the customer. Integrate the PIC into the next generation of office products, within the next 24–30 months.
Projected Start/ End Dates	Start Date: 06/09 End Date: 06/10
Resources Requirements	Design Team (5 managers @ 75% of time commitment) Integration Team (3 managers @ 30% time commitment)
Risk Assessment	Total Requested: $1.25 million. Supplier quality and delivery of materials may not meet standards (conduct supplier risk assessment). Sales could fall short of estimate (expect to break even with sales to existing customer base). Price point and contribution margins to be determined.
Financial Opportunity	Year 1: $3 million Year 2: $4.5 million

Exhibit 4-7. Sample template to guide planning and execution (continued)

Manager's Checklist for Chapter 4

☑ Understand how execution fits into strategy and business plan deployment.

☑ Compare execution and deployment tools such as Balanced Scorecards and Hoshin Planning.

☑ Use execution and deployment tools to organize key objectives and measurements.

☑ Assess your readiness for execution.

☑ Populate execution and deployment tools with your company data.

Mobilizing the Workforce

've mentioned several times that to be successful in developing and executing a plan, interaction is a must. The Management by Objectives systems of the past failed largely because they were individually focused, highly structured, and rigid, and lacked good interaction and flexibility to work in organizations.

The engagement and mobilization of the workforce is the linking mechanism in terms of detailed action planning and execution of the plan. Whether a company is capital- or labor-intensive, it will still rely on people to carry out plans and make day-to-day decisions. The thinking here is that to effectively mobilize the workforce, three building blocks are necessary:

1. A culture or set of behaviors that support the achievement of the plans.
2. An effective communication process with both formal and informal components.
3. A structured process to link the planning tools to the people or the business cascade, as we are calling it here.

Creating the Right Business Culture to Produce the Results

One way to think about culture is that it's "the way people behave." A company culture can be considered the sum total of these behaviors.

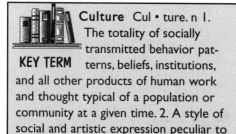

Culture Cul • ture. n 1. The totality of socially transmitted behavior patterns, beliefs, institutions, and all other products of human work and thought typical of a population or community at a given time. 2. A style of social and artistic expression peculiar to a class or society.

KEY TERM

Simply stated, culture is the "way we do things," as described by Martin Bower, former chairman of McKinsey and Co.

Organizations have unique cultures that are expressed in the way people talk, think, and act. Culture is a product of company history, policies, and beliefs, both stated and unstated; it is embodied in the personal attributes of company leaders past and present. The benefits of a focused culture are that the expected behaviors are geared to assisting the organization to reach its business results. The thinking here is that the culture should be shaped to ensure that the right behaviors are in place that drive the business forward.

Shaping Culture

Every company has a culture that defines it. In some cases, subcultures may exist in companies that may differ from the predominant culture. The major point here is that companies have an opportunity to shape their cultures to create the "right" behavioral attributes needed to achieve successful business results. To shape a culture, you must define the required cultural attributes.

You can often do this by preparing a list of the most important behaviors that will contribute to business success. This effort could be an extension of delineating company values and linking them directly to the needs of the business.

Alternatively, you should identify gaps by comparing the current cultural attributes to the new requirements. A significant concern regarding the current culture is that many of these attributes have become the established ways of thinking and behaving. In some cases, there may be a need to shift a culture to meet changing business demands. The box on the next page shows a few examples of these shifts.

From	To
Hierarchical structures	Flatter structures
Functional units	Matrix structures
Individual focus	Team-based focus
Technology awareness	Technology proficiency

The implications for some will be to acquire new ways of thinking about the way they work in the required business environment. The following information may assist you in shaping or shifting culture.

Using Cultural Influences to Shape Culture

Use of cultural influences, such as policies and work practices, company history, symbols and rituals, training and education, and leadership, can have a strong impact on shaping a company culture. Use these influences to create a sense of company norms and reinforce the desired cultural attributes, while eliminating unproductive or counterproductive behaviors.

Synergy Culture may be considered the sum total of the individual behaviors in an organization. The impact **KEY TERM** of synergy on an organization is the power to make the whole or outputs greater than the sum of the individual parts. Synergy is achieved by sharing and complementing skills, insights, and overall abilities to work together to solve problems and achieve business results. The purpose of defining the cultural attributes is to help organizations achieve synergy by guiding the behaviors of individuals to focus on what is needed from them.

Mapping Business and Organizational Strategies with Cultural Attributes

The following box outlines an approach for mapping organizational strategies with the organization's cultural atrributes.

Annual Business Strategies
- Launch new products ahead of the competition
- Increase market share
- Improve product and service quality
- Initiate cost reduction programs

Organizational Strategies
- Flat structures
- Focused decision making (at lowest possible level)
- Team-based environment (cross-business and cross-functional)

Implications for the Required Cultural Attributes
- Sense of urgency
- Collaborative mindset
- Customer focused
- Financially focused
- Competitive mindset

How Culture Attributes Can Drive Business Results

An example of a culture shift occurred with the deregulation in industries such as utilities and telecommunications. With the onset of deregulation, the operating environments changed to ones in which customers had choices of suppliers and fixed prices for services were being phased out. The mandates for change were not an option. For some companies, it meant redefining the way business would be conducted and changing the required behaviors for employees to be successful. New attributes that appeared in this environment included being competitively minded and financially focused. Managers gave employees much more information regarding the company's financial performance and expected them to be more responsive to customers and flexible in learning best practices to make the company more competitive.

Shifting the Business Culture

German-born psychologist Kurt Lewin was one of the first researchers to study group dynamics and organizational development. In managing change, Lewin classified the change process into three steps: unfreezing, moving, and refreezing. In applying this model to shifting a business culture, we can use the present stage, the transition stage, and the desired stage. Consider that the current stage represents the current culture and the transition stage is the moving toward the required culture by applying cultural influences to reach the desired stage, as shown in Exhibit 5-1.

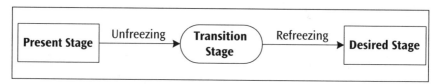

Exhibit 5-1. Applying the Lewin model to make a culture shift

To apply this model appropriately, a process of re-education and establishment of company norms is required. Essentially, a clear presentation of the desired stage or required attributes will provide the launch point for the business case for making the cultural shift. A powerful way to do this is in the deployment process, as outlined in the succeeding business cascade.

A Communication System Strengthens Culture

One of the most important aspects of execution of business strategies and plans is the communication system in place to facilitate the planning, actions, and reporting of progress during the business year. The effectiveness of communication will enable more accurate data gathering and allow for more timely decisions. This will be especially effective in times of change when swift analysis and adjustments may mean the survival of an organization.

A recent example occurred in a manufacturing company whose major competitor introduced a new product that immediately took market share from its existing products. The challenge of this company was how to mobilize its marketing, design, engineering, and manufacturing teams to come up with an immediate response to this threat.

The key to building an effective communication system involves two elements. The first is the structure of the system itself with a process to guide information flow. The second element is the people in the system and their abilities to use good communication practices and avoid the communication pitfalls facing organizations today.

Common Communication System Pitfalls

Organizational communication has been an enormous challenge, especially in companies that have grown and have multiple locations. As we discuss building an effective

> **Communicate** According to the dictionary: 1. To impart; pass along; transmit; to make known; 2. To give and receive information, signals or messages in any way.
>
> **KEY TERM**
>
> The major missing link in today's fast-paced organizations is the ability to close the communication loop, from sender to receiver, and make the communication interaction truly two-way. This is implied in the quote from Gregory Bateson, "Communication is information that makes a difference."

communication system, it's worth noting the pitfalls that must be remedied for success.

- Reliance on technology such as voice mail and electronic mail versus face-to-face contacts whenever possible.
- Lack of communication about policies and guidelines.
- Lack of reach to isolated groups who may be separated in multiple locations or by shift differences.
- Lack of feedback and follow-up and missed opportunities to close the loop on recommended actions.
- Lack of ability to control information in a rapidly changing environment.

SMART

MANAGING

Skip Level Communication

Many gaps exist in the communication system. One glaring gap is the disconnection between company management and employees who may be three or four levels below them. A technique called Skip Level Communication has been developed to close this gap. This process involves managers going down to the next level or in some cases, two levels or more to engage employees. The purpose of this communication technique is to obtain feedback on the effectiveness of formal company communications and to use this forum as a platform to answer questions and gather suggestions for improvements.

How People Get Information

Research has confirmed that the most effective method of communication is through the immediate supervisor. The immediate supervisor has the most direct contact with their employees, and employees expect and want to get information from their supervisors. Other techniques that have impact on communications include small group meetings, executive presentations, newsletters, and use of electronic media such as e-mail and electronic learning programs. To ensure that employees have the information they need to make appropriate decisions and do their jobs, a multifaceted approach is required.

The Communication System Framework

Communications should flow to all levels of the company. The methods of communication should provide timely information as the formal system.

The levels must also be linked by an information subsystem of feedback and two-way communications. In the framework displayed in Exhibit 5-2, several communication methods are integrated within the flow of information. One company initiated a telephone hotline where employees could call and leave a message regarding a concern or suggestion that they wished to voice to company management. Responses to anonymous messages were posted on the company website. If a person left a name, they were contacted directly by a member of the company management.

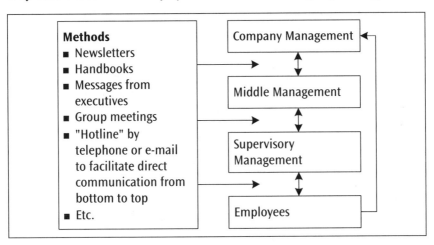

Exhibit 5-2. Communication system framework

SMART

COMMUNICATING IN TIMES OF CHANGE

MANAGING

Conventional wisdom tells us that communication must increase during times of change and chaos. In fact, if communication were doubled in terms of frequency, that would be about right in turbulent and chaotic times. The main purpose of the communication is to provide real-time information, even if it's incomplete. The value of communication is twofold. First, it provides a clear message as to what is actually taking place, in both good times and bad times. Second, the communication nullifies the grapevine communications that often carry distorted or inaccurate information.

Business Cascade

Considering that the cultural and communication frameworks have been established, there is a high readiness factor for the deployment of the company business strategies and aligning those in the functional plans. The business cascade is an effective way to engage and mobilize the workforce to complete these plans so that their individual performance can be finalized as well. The main focus is to assemble professional and supervisory personnel so they have a common understanding and commitment to the direction, strategies, and major objectives of the company and so they can, in turn, link this information to next-level plans.

Think of the business cascade as an elevator shaft. If you are standing at the bottom, you can look up and see the connections to the other floors. In a similar way, the business cascade is a framework in which every person can look up and see the connections to the next level of planning (Exhibit 5-3). This can help create the feeling that every level is critical to the achievement of the company objectives (and every level is).

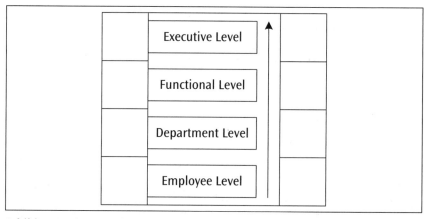

Exhibit 5-3. The view from the elevator shaft

The business cascade can be used in two stages. The goal of the first stage is to introduce the company strategies and business objectives through the use of the Balanced Scorecard, Hoshin Planning, or other deployment tools as outlined in Chapter 4. The information presented here should be clarified with questions and input from the cascade participants. The goal of this stage is to use the company's high-level input to assist in finalizing the functional and individual performance plans.

Stage 1 Business Cascade

Stage 1 business cascade meetings can last anywhere from two to four hours, depending on the size of the group and the detailed questions and interactions required to clarify the information presented. All questions must be resolved either during the meeting or shortly thereafter so the next-level planning can successfully take place.

Audience. All supervisory and professional personnel.

Meeting Structure. The first business cascade should have two parts: The first part is a presentation of the company deployment tool, such as the Balanced Scorecard or Hoshin Plan. During the presentation the meeting leader, typically the functional leader, takes notes and addresses questions that arise regarding the information presented. As part of this presentation, the cultural attributes are reviewed. If the company wishes to use its stated values in lieu of cultural attributes, then a discussion can ensue regarding how the functional team can make them a reality as they deploy the plans and in their day-to-day interactions.

The second part of the meeting should be a roundtable discussion to answer the following questions:

- How can our function impact the financial performance of the company?
- What can our function do to improve service to our customers?
- How can we participate in the cost reduction emphasis of the company?
- What other impacts can we have related to the company strategies and focus areas for this year?
- How can we "bring alive" the cultural attributes and/or company values?

Planning Tools. Balanced Scorecard, Hoshin planning table, or other presentation of the company strategies and focus areas.

Stage 2 Business Cascade

Stage 2 business cascade meetings are dedicated to completing functional plans and to feeding individual performance plans. It's imperative to present a preliminary framework for this plan that can be fine-tuned and used by each team member to finalize their individual plans. The tool selected here is designed to link the Balanced Scorecards to functional plans. This will ensure that these plans are integrated prior to completion of individual plans.

POSTER SESSIONS

TOOLS   One technique to encourage input and participation during the cascade meetings is to have the participants write their comments on sticky notes and post them on a wall or flip chart or wall chart at various points during the meeting. An opportunity to apply this technique comes after the presentation of the company Balanced Scorecard information. The Balanced Scorecard format can be enlarged to poster size and attached to a wall in the meeting room. On a break, participants are asked to use sticky notes to make comments, ask questions, or make suggestions. The meeting leader can use this information to prepare a response or to further refine the presentation for clarity.

RULES OF ENGAGEMENT

TOOLS   Employee engagement is not an initiative or program. Rather, it's an ongoing process of communication, feedback, and measurement of progress against the established plans. Participation is the key to success. People like to be part of the objective-setting process and will work harder toward objectives they had a hand in creating. Participation should begin with the business cascade and continue through the individual work planning and appraisal stages.

Audience. All supervisory and professional personnel.

Meeting Structure. This is a half-day planning meeting, starting with the review of the Balanced Scorecard Deployment Worksheet, which illustrates the linkages to the overall company strategies and objectives. The remainder of this meeting is dedicated to drafting the next level of plans by further developing the functional objectives into department and individual plans.

Planning Tools. The business cascade using the strategy deployment worksheet (Exhibit 5-4) is an excellent way to ensure that the company strategies and objectives are aligned with the functional key results and objectives. Once this has been accomplished, the next-level planning can be undertaken. Using the Departmental and Individual Planning Form, the last step in the cascade can begin. Work will be needed outside the second-stage cascade meeting to finalize the next-level plans. Checkmarks are placed in the boxes that align with strategies when the key results and objectives are in support of them. If the key results and objectives support a major objective, that's written in. The worksheet captures the measurement technique to be employed to monitor progress. The completed worksheet in Exhibit 5-4 is an example.

Vision: The company will achieve commanding leadership in all segments in which it competes and be a recognized world-class organization.

	Strategies				Major Objectives	
	#1	**#2**	**#3**	**#4**	Financial	
	Increase on-time deliveries to 97%	Become a world-class organization	Increase productivity by 5% annually	Strengthen core capabilities	Sales and Operating Income Targets People Retention Rate Customer Market Share Targets Internal Processes New Product Development Speed	
Functional Key Results Areas and Objectives						**Measurment and Tracking Technique**
Reduce Customer Complaints					Customer Retention	Check sheet Pareto Chart
Reduce Supplier Costs and Lead Times	✔					Flowchart Customer-- Supplier Worksheet
Increase Sales Volume and Profitability						P & L Statement
Reduce Involuntary Turnover		✔				Monthly Reports

Exhibit 5-4. Business cascade–strategy deployment worksheet

USING THE DEPARTMENTAL AND INDIVIDUAL PLANNING FORM

Key Results Areas and Functional Objectives for Supply Chain Management

- Reduce supplier costs and lead times
- Reduce total cycle time (order to shipment) by 20%

TOOLS

> - Increase supplier quality from dock to stock to 95%
> - Reduce direct material costs by 10%
>
> **Departmental/Individual Objectives in Support of the Functional Objectives**
> - Using the information in Chapter 3, complete the next-level objective setting
>
> **Measurement Tools**
> - Using the information in the Appendix, select the measurement tools

Information Management

Information management and information technology are increasingly significant and continue to make tremendous changes in the way organizations conduct business. The management of planning information will contribute greatly to the accuracy of the plans and to accelerating decision making in an organization. In many organizations, the finance function has taken the responsibility for collecting planning information related to the fixed annual budget and profit and loss statements, which will become important yardsticks of business performance. Several iterations of this information may be required before it's finalized. The statements can be reviewed monthly by all functional leaders and cascaded down the organization to ensure that all managers who have financial responsibility of any kind will be able to view their financial performance. This also opens up the opportunity to make adjustments as required. This will be discussed in detail in Chapter 7.

Training

Training has been successfully used to increase employee knowledge and skills while facilitating the deployment of company strategies and plans. Every training session related to this effort should include three important processes: review and reinforce the strategies, review and reinforce the cultural attributes required for success, and deliver specific skills that will help employees execute the strategies and plans. Following are a few examples of training programs that have helped to mobilize workforces.

Financial Excellence

Many companies have developed training programs and workshops that focus on how each person can impact the company's financial performance. One company developed a program for all managers called "Know the Numbers" in which all company managers were trained on all financial statements such as the income statement, balance sheet, and cash flow statement. The program included a definition of key terms and ratios as well as exercises on how the managers could impact the numbers from their position in the company, from both the revenue-producing and support roles.

Productivity and Quality at the Source of the Work

Mobilizing the workforce should reach every level of the organization. A quality principle is that productivity and quality are controlled at the source of the work, not by a supervisor but by the individuals who perform the work. In many organizations, increasing productivity is high on the list of strategies because it makes the organization more effective. These improvements of even 5% or more can have a dramatic impact on operating income and ultimately make the organization more competitive in the marketplace.

To this end, Lean Techniques have emerged as part of the Six Sigma Program or as foundation training for employees as a prelude to such key tools as Business Process Improvement and Value Stream Mapping. The 6 S Audit (sort, simplify, sweep, standardize, self-discipline, and safety) is widely accepted as a method of organizing the workplace and contributing significantly to continuous improvement and productivity gains. These techniques provide tools to those individuals closest to the work so they can participate and help control quality and productivity.

The 6 S is considered the "foundation for everything" and instructs employees on how to follow these procedures to improve their workplaces and individual productivity.

- **Sorting** is the proper arrangement of everything that is touched in each work area. This will eliminate clutter and unnecessary items. Sorting also reviews all items in common areas that must be arranged to mutual benefit and access.

- **Simplifying** is the determination of the exact location for each item in individual and common areas. This will allow for better organization and more productive use of these items.
- **Sweeping** is the identification of problems in the work areas such as unsafe conditions or broken/malfunctioning equipment. This will allow for the immediate resolution of these issues.
- **Standardizing** is the establishment of work flows and use of simple systems to determine how the work is done. Visual systems and job aids work well.
- **Self-Discipline** is the attitude to constantly look for ways to improve every aspect of the work area.
- **Safety** is the relentless pursuit of safe working conditions, safety practices, and prevention of accidents.

Kaizen

The Kaizen Event takes three to five days and focuses on the most critical business process—manufacturing or service—to get significant levels of productivity, quality, and profits. A team of 6 to 12 people from across the organization is formed and given one full day of training in techniques to identify and eliminate waste. The team spends the rest of its time implementing the new, improved process.

At the conclusion of the Kaizen Event, not only has a key business process been quickly improved, but a team has been trained that can apply this same technique to other processes in the company. The benefits of Kaizen include:

- Providing quick implementation.
- Low cost since it relies on your own people.
- Creating an effective team approach to problem solving and process improvement.
- Discovering the sources of duplication, unnecessary steps, and waste in the processes and permanently eliminating them, which improves the process and adds value to the customer.

Manager's Checklist for Chapter 5

☑ Determine if your company culture is focused on getting business results.

☑ Gain an understanding of how to shape and shift cultural attributes.

☑ Develop a communication system that supports the timely delivery of information.

☑ Identify the components of a business cascade.

☑ Use a business cascade to drive business strategy and functional plans.

☑ Use training to empower and mobilize the workforce, including the 6 S Lean Techniques.

☑ Evaluate your ability to manage information, especially with respect to prividing timely financial updates.

Tracking, Controlling, and Reviewing the Plans

L et's take a quick look back at the information presented in this book thus far. Assume that the planning flow has been followed as prescribed in Chapter 1, including the link from a strategic view of the business to the annual business plan. A Balanced Scorecard organizes the key company objectives and broad measurements so that they can be cascaded throughout the organization. Functional plans are prepared and finalized, aligning this information with individual performance standards. Other work of the organization may also be carried out through initiatives and projects that may cross functional lines. If this has been the case, alignment has occurred.

As the business year is launched and underway, there are important checkpoints during the year to ensure that the plans are on track to achieve the results that were committed to. It's the responsibility of the company executives and functional management to provide the mechanisms to track the results and report progress on a monthly and quarterly basis. This chapter is dedicated to developing a system to accomplish this task.

Planning versus Tracking and Controlling

Planning takes place within designated timeframes during the business year and focuses on establishing the objectives and plans that will drive the business forward. Tracking and controlling activities are ongoing

TOOLS

CODING

One method of creating a visual for status reporting is to use a coding system for each objective included in a functional plan. Color coding is a popular method and uses the colors of green—on time, yellow—caution, and red—behind schedule. This is a way of using the colors to identify issues in the yellow and red areas and provide some explanation of what is causing the caution or delay. Coding systems expedite the review process because they can focus discussions on what needs to be done to get performance on track for success.

and focus on providing timely information that measures the progress of the plans.

Creating a Management System

A management system is a powerful tool because it provides the visibility and opportunity to control the essential components of meeting objectives. This system will assist in ensuring that the function and supporting departments meet their commitments to the company.

Purposes of a Management System

The purposes of a management system include:

- Provides controls and ability to monitor progress.
- Supports the integration of company objectives with functional plans.
- Ensures that managers have planning and management tools that give real-time information to improve the quality of decision making.
- Creates better time management by allowing managers to focus on the most critical issues.
- Helps avoid surprises.

TOOLS

72/45 RULE

When reviewing progress against the planned objectives, issues and concerns will arise. Once the issue has been identified, corrective action must be initiated within 72 hours to ensure that the issue has a chance to be addressed to minimize negative impact on the business. In addition, the follow-up and implementation of corrective actions must occur within 45 days of the correction action plan to be successful.

The key areas of tracking and monitoring progress will focus on objectives and measurements developed in the functional plan. The major grouping includes:

Operations. In the tracking of day-to-day operations, the focus is on quantity, quality, timeliness, and cost. In addition, a measurement of customer satisfaction should be included. These customers can be external, internal, or both. Exhibit 6-1 shows a form for tracking operations.

Objective	Measurement	How Tracked	Control	Corrective Action (As required)
Effectively manage labor costs	Within 5% of monthly budget amount	Weekly labor report	Actual vs. budget	

Exhibit 6-1. Tracking operations

Process Management. The core business processes should be monitored, using the Chapter 3 measurements that were converted from the voice of the customer (VOC). A monthly review of these measurements will quickly identify to what extent the process is adding value to the customer.

Business Initiative/Project Management. The measurements established in the approval process will be excellent indicators of the progress being made. The best tracking tool is the Gantt chart (page 95) for monitoring performance including start, progress, and end dates.

REDUCING THE COST OF SALES   **SMART**

The view of every cost center manager who has budget responsibility should be that they affect the cost of sales for every decision they make. This impact can come from controlling direct selling expenses such as shipping, discounts, and allowances. In addition,   **MANAGING** every expense that can be reduced, even as a general expense, can lower the cost of sales. This continuous improvement mentality will pay dividends to the organization because it will help to maintain competitiveness and contribute to increasing margins on both products and services.

Objective and Project Tracking

The monitoring and tracking of the objectives and projects will provide ongoing progress reports to the departments and functional managers, and will be critical to evaluate progress against plan in the quarterly and annual reviews (to be addressed later in this chapter). Computer software is available to do this, but some may want to use a simple tracking tool similar to that shown in Exhibit 6-2. The objective tracking form used in conjunction with a Gantt chart will serve this purpose.

Objective _____				
Category: _____ Maintenance _____ Improvement _____ Other				
Step Number	Major Action Steps	Dates Start End	Measurement Criteria	Comments

Exhibit 6-2. Objective tracking form

Objective Tracking Form

The main purpose of the objective tracking form is to outline the steps required to achieve the objective or complete the project. Each step is detailed with the actions needed to complete the step. A start and end date are estimated so that tracking can be done visually with a Gantt chart. Measurement criteria will also indicate how well the action steps are being completed. Reporting by exceptions or when you have exceeded or fallen below expectations is a good method for focusing attention on the highs and lows of performance.

The Gantt chart monitors the complete schedule of an objective or project. Once the steps are sequenced, they can be tracked and monitored by using the status reporting legend. If maintained properly, the Gantt chart can be an accurate way to determine progress, especially if problems occur (Exhibit 6-3).

People and Performance Management. Using the performance standards and measurements established in Chapter 3, performance plans should be monitored on a quarterly basis and can be coupled with the ongoing

Objective Project Name	Start Date	End Date	% Complete	Status	Jan	Feb	Mar	Apr	May	Jun	Jul	Aug	Sep	Oct	Nov	Dec
														Comments		

Legend
- - - - - Work Scheduled
———— Work Completed
◄ Target Completion Date
► Actual Completion Date

Legend
On Time: Work is on schedule as of current date
Ahead: Work ahead of schedule as of current date
Late: Active project behind schedule as of current date
Complete: Project complete
Unscheduled: No activity originally scheduled during period
Delay: Activity postponed as of current date
Delete: Project has been cancelled

Exhibit 6-3. Tracking with a Gantt chart

business reviews outlined in this chapter. It's also useful to have individuals prepare a short monthly progress report, noting exceptions with respect to falling behind or moving ahead of expectations, schedules, or measurements.

Influencing the Essentials

An industrial products company recently established customer response as a key company objective for the business year. Several different departments were involved with this objective, and it was established as a priority in the functional plans. The company objective was for 95% on-time deliveries. In one of the subplant units, a manager reviewed the VOC feedback and set up a tracking and control process to ensure that this objective was met. After converting the VOC requirements into measurements, the target was that the delivery was received on the date specified and within two hours of a specific delivery time. The next step was to set a baseline performance, which was the actual on-time delivery performance to date. In using this scenario, the manager was able to set up the following tracking system:

Objective	Baseline	Measurement	Control	Corrective Action (As required)
Meet on-time delivery schedule at 95%	Current performance at 92%	97% Exceed 95% Target <95% Below	Weekly delivery report % (actual vs. target)	

If the control report indicated the actual performance was below the target of 95%, an immediate investigation was begun. This is the first step in the corrective action. The complete corrective action process includes the following steps:

1. Investigate the situation. Identify the issues causing the deficiency. Create a problem statement.
2. Select and define improvement opportunities.
3. Analyze root causes of the problem.
4. Select the best solution.
5. Test the solution—trial implementation.

> **World-class organization** There are any number of metrics that can define a world-class organization, one that is among the best in the world in terms of its products, services, and industry standing. The best-in-class organizations achieve their **KEY TERM** positions by going beyond best practices when setting objectives and targets. The goal of these world-class organizations is to go beyond industry standards and to be recognized as a leader to their customers. This is accomplished by setting breakthrough objectives and targets that go beyond the incremental improvements such as 5 to 10%.

6. Implement the solution.
7. Track the effectiveness with the controls identified.

In carrying out these steps, use the appropriate problem-solving tools (see Appendix), such as brainstorming, cause and effect diagrams, action plans, etc. A detailed guide to corrective action is also included in the Appendix to this book.

The Review Process

Business reviews should be conducted with the timeline presented in Chapter 1 and repeated here. Quarterly reviews are most common unless some major unplanned events are having negative impacts on the company performance. The quarterly reviews will focus on the business performance related to the income statement, or profit and loss statement. Balance sheets and cash flow data are also reviewed at the highest level for consistency with the overall strategic and business plan objectives. The goal of these reviews is to study the numbers, explain the situation, and tell a story about the business performance thus far. One important comparison point is how the company is tracking against the market trends. This will help to validate the forecast for the remaining portion of the business year. In some situations, it may mean a re-forecasting process is indicated. Exhibit 6-4 shows the timeline for this process.

Conducting the Quarterly Business Review

The quarterly business review should focus on key areas of performance to key measurements, budget, forecast vs. actual results, and trends that may affect the business. The trends may be positive or negative, and you should review them in light of industry performance. In addition, a

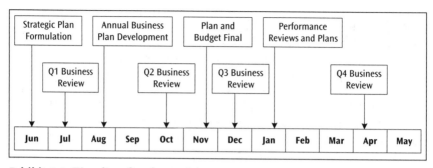

Exhibit 6-4. Timeline for the review process

review of the major projects and initiatives by function should be completed to ensure progress is being made and to recheck that business priorities have not changed so significantly that they would warrant a change in the direction of any of the projects or initiatives.

DASHBOARDS

TOOLS

Many companies use dashboards or displays that create a visual review of daily, weekly, and monthly performance based on selected measurements. Dashboards can be as simple as using a white board to display the information. Other options include use of a bulletin board to exhibit status reports and updates for all employees to read. A few companies are using ticker tape displays of overall company performance, including stock prices and sales updates. The main purpose of the dashboards is to highlight the information so that everyone knows where the performance stands at that point in time.

Income Statement

Top Level Revenue

– Cost of Goods Sold

= Gross Margin

Questions:

- Did the company revenues achieve the quarterly targets?
- How did this performance compare to the same period last year?
- Are there any historical trends that are impacting these results?
- Were there any issues in the cost of goods sold that need to be corrected (looking at any discounts and allowances that may have impacted the results)?

- Were the gross margin dollars and percentages at the acceptable level as planned?
- How did this performance compare to the same period last year?

Gross Margin
– Operating Expenses
= Operating Income

Questions:

- Were the expenses within 5% of budget?
- Was the operating income at the target for the quarter met?
- What extraordinary expenses have occurred during the quarter?
- Are there any worrisome trends that must be addressed?

Functional Review

Sales and marketing report on:

- Top-line sales: broken out by product or service lines
- Product mix: profitability by product line or service lines
- Selling costs: impact on profitability

Operations report on:

- Output: ship dollars
- Cost: materials and labor
- Quality: scrap and reject rates
- Operation improvements: process and project management

Support functions report on:

- Performance to budget: within 5%
- Major objectives and projects: performance to schedule
- Other notable developments

Quarterly Individual Performance Reviews

The quarterly individual performance reviews are essentially feedback reviews on progress against objectives. This is an opportunity to ensure that individual performance plans are on track for successful completion, and if they're not on track, midcourse corrections can be made. Coding and exception reporting play an important role in identifying those areas that may be cautionary or behind in schedule.

Conducting Successful Individual Performance Reviews

The consensus among employees is that they dread their performance reviews because they're too often surprised with the feedback they receive. The main reason for this is that performance plans are poorly prepared and don't provide an objective starting point for both periodic feedback and the annual performance review. If the business planning processes outlined in this book are followed, including the links between company and functional and individual plans, much of the negative perception of this process can be eliminated.

Employee-Centered Coaching Model

Employee-centered coaching shifts the responsibility for preparing a performance feedback session and presenting an update to a supervisor for review and comments. In preparing for this session, the individual should use the performance standards prepared at the start of the business year as the foundation for the meeting. The main premise in using this model is that an employee will likely be aware of strengths and improvement areas and it's a positive start to a discussion when the person responsible for their performance has an opportunity to tell a story, versus being told about their performance by the supervisor. The supervisor can be more effective as a coach during this process.

You can facilitate the employee-centered coaching model in the following manner.

DISCUSSION MODEL
1. Employee leads with success regarding performance standards.
2. Supervisor reinforces.
3. Supervisor adds any positive inputs/feedback.
4. Employee discusses any issues of setbacks.
5. Supervisor notes and gives feedback about making improvements.
6. *Blind Spot:* Supervisor adds any corrective feedback not discussed by the employee.

Employees will recognize, on average, about 75% of their successes and issues for improvement. Recognition on their part will maximize and facilitate the coaching ability of the manager to reinforce their comments and to add required corrective feedback. This will ensure a commitment to improvement for the future.

Organizational Reviews

Organizational reviews are conducted on an annual cycle. They are structured to present the alignment of the function and how the human resources are positioned to help achieve

Feedback To be effective, feedback must give specific information that can reinforce or change behavior. **KEY TERM** Feedback should not be judgmental and must focus on the specific issues or situation, not the person. Feedback should be two-way. The feedback giver can present the information and must allow the feedback receiver to respond so that the complete story can be determined. This is the starting point for improvement, especially in those situations where corrective action is required.

the objectives and plans. This segment of the organizational review also focuses on succession planning with the goal of identifying both replacements and potential promotions to fill future vacancies. This is often referred to as "bench strength" because it can ensure that the organization has the talent in place when needed to drive the business forward.

Organizational Review Format—Four Key Sections

Last 12 Months' Changes in Organization. The purpose of this section is to highlight the major changes that have occurred with respect to personnel, including promotions, changes in responsibility, and turnover (voluntary and involuntary). The change in personnel can have an impact on the organization's ability to deliver products and services if openings aren't filled quickly and if skill gaps remain.

Current Organization Chart to Future Organization Chart. The purpose of this section is to demonstrate how the organization is structured to achieve its objectives and plans. The future organization is a projection of a new structure that can improve product and service delivery in the future. If major changes are indicated here, a transition plan should be included.

Succession Plan. The purpose of this section is to identify replacements for all management personnel and plans for developing individuals with potential to take higher levels of responsibility within the next one to three years. Specific positions and training required should be documented. This approach to having a "bench" available can be an answer to the changes in personnel that will occur from time to time. With the onset of baby boomer retirement, there is a concern that leadership talent needs will increase dramatically over the next few years. Developing internal talent will be critical to the future of every organization.

Issues or Challenges That Must Be Addressed. In closing, any other issues that may be potential roadblocks should be documented, which may include shortages of technical skills and competencies, retirements, and the potential for loss of key talent.

CAUTION

THE BLAME GAME

A natural tendency can often impede the tracking process and correction of problems. Often managers will feel compelled to assign blame for an issue, rather than taking the approach of fixing the problem. It's the responsibility of every manager to be proactive in identifying issues and to engage in immediate problem definition and problem-solving actions. If the issue is cross-functional in nature, it may be necessary to bring in the next level of management to help coordinate a solution. This will eliminate the "silo" (or isolation) effect where planning and problem solving are self-contained and may miss the opportunity for longer-term, cross-functional solutions to problems.

Business Planning Retreats

Conducting business planning retreats can be a productive way to communicate company objectives, cultural attributes/values, and overall plans in a forum that facilitates the integration of this information to multiple levels in the organization. These planning retreats are most effective when used in combination with presentations and smaller group breakout sessions for discussion and more detailed planning. It's an opportunity to share the high-level business organizers such as a Balanced Scorecard and to use this tool to launch functional planning. In essence, this can be considered a high-level cascade of information and can serve as a model for other managers to use in rolling out this information in their areas of responsibility.

Planning Retreat Format

Following is a sample format for planning a retreat. Retreats can last from one to three days, depending on the size of the group and how deeply the planning process will go. Retreats are usually held outside the company facility and may require the participants to stay an evening in a hotel. If this format is employed, a group dinner and team-building activities can be excellent methods of unifying the group around the company plans.

TYPICAL AGENDA

Welcome: Keynote Opening from Company President/CEO

Company Vision, Strategies, Objectives, and Values (Cultural Attributes)

Facilitated Discussion: What are our challenges going forward?

Functional Presentations: Mission and priorities for the business year

Balanced Scorecard Presentation

Functional Planning: Subgroup exercise

Team-Building Event (optional)

Wrap-Up

Closing Ceremony

SIGN-ON CEREMONY

Sign-on or sign-up ceremonies can impact the motivation of a group to work toward common objectives. This unified commitment is an important characteristic of a high-performing team and will be a building block for communication and shared commitment to both individual and company performance. Usually done at the end of the session, the sign-on provides a visible sign of the team members by having every person sign a document together. This can be done on a poster for all to see.

FOR EXAMPLE

Case Study: The Equipment Division

Company History. It all started back in the 1920s with a couple of guys who had a better idea, and in those days that was all it took to start a business. They began by manufacturing small equipment and parts that were not readily available in the local market. It was not long before they had built a steady business.

During WWI and WWII, they were able to adapt their products to wartime needs and were able to build a sizable government contract. This revenue stream provided the capital needed to expand and add manufacturing space. Although they had some ups and downs, the company continued to grow and build a reputation for high quality in everything they produced.

After WWII, they were well-positioned to take advantage of the prosperity of the 1950s and 1960s. They continued to expand, and by 1965, built a national distribution network. By the end of the decade they had several high-end and specialty products that were in high demand, especially in the building and construction industry.

Acquisition Mania. In the early 1970s, the company was purchased by a large industrial firm that pumped cash into its newest division. Growth continued into the early 1980s, when a couple of the executives were able to successfully orchestrate a leveraged buyout. They liked the potential of the business and set their sights on expanding product lines that supported the retail construction industry.

In the late 1980s, the equipment division changed hands twice! The "big boys" seemed to think that the potential of this business was unlimited, given the growing market and continued demand for the products.

Life Is Good. Business in the late 1980s and early 1990s was good. All the competitors were "playing in their own sandboxes." The equipment division was positioned nicely in the retail market it had established over the years. There were a few niche players, but that didn't impact them much. In fact, price increases of 5 to 10% each year were commonplace.

There were a few problems. Quality slipped and shipments were too often late. No showstoppers, though. The brand still remained strong.

Wake-Up Call. Who said that the 1990s would be different? Well, that prediction rang true for the equipment division.

Life sure changed. The economy remained stable overall, but outside factors even beyond competition began to impact the business. The EPA passed legislation that banned a harmful raw material that was being used heavily in the products. And if that wasn't enough, the parent company was exerting major pressure, with the spotlight on profitability and efficiency. Each operating division was expected to hit aggressive targets each year as part of their strategic plan.

The key divisional objectives focused on the following areas and indicators:

1. **Product Development Speed:** Reduce cycle times by 25%, from 12 to 9 months.
2. **Cost of Raw Materials:** Reduce overall costs from $750K to $600K.
3. **On-Time Deliveries:** Increase on-time deliveries from 88% to 95%.

All of this now became the price of admission to defend their position in the changing marketplace.

You Make the Call. The company has hired you as an outside consultant to examine the problems recently identified and advise them on a course of action. The company will depend on you to help fix a long-term problem. Although objectives have been set each year, it seems that the ongoing measure of success has been lacking. The discipline of tracking and monitoring results needs to be modeled for them.

As you begin your work on helping to determine where the company stands on the three key objectives, you'll want to address the following questions:

- What data should be collected?
- What format should be used to collect the data and how often?
- How will the data be reported to the company management?

Complete the template below, using the information provided in this chapter to guide your responses.

Product Development Speed to Market Reduce cycle times by 25%, from 12 to 9 months	Data Collected and Tracked	How Reported
Cost of Raw Materials Reduce overall costs from $750K to $600K		
On-Time Deliveries Increase on-time deliveries from 88% to 95%		

Manager's Checklist for Chapter 6

☑ Understand the key elements of tracking and monitoring plans.

☑ Use a management system to set up a tracking program.

☑ Apply tracking tools, such as objective tracking forms and Gantt charts.

☑ Use guidelines on how to conduct business and individual performance reviews.

☑ Create an organization review.

☑ Facilitate planning retreats to expedite integration of reviews.

☑ Create a tracking format customizable to your business.

Chapter

7

Contingency Planning

Many economists and futurists predicted that doing business in the new millennium would be different. Through the tragic events of the terrorist attacks on September 11, 2001, both personal loss and economic impacts gripped the United States. Industry downturns created loss of revenues for many companies, especially in travel-related services. Corporate fraud and scandals have littered the business landscape, now global in nature. The impact on companies has been devastating, and it demands that companies prepare for risks and make adjustments to their overall strategies and plans going forward.

What's Changing?

Over the past 20 years many of the companies in the Fortune 500 ranks have been acquired, merged with other companies, or gone out of business. Part of the reason for these situations is an inability to deal with changing market conditions and to make the adjustments required for survival.

Changes You Have Seen

In thinking about the marketplace in which you work and conduct business, think about the changes you have personally seen in the past five years with regard to the following.

Customers. The most common changes cited by managers were customers who demanded more regarding pricing and on-time deliveries. Because their customers have become less predictable, there's an increasing requirement for just-in-time deliveries. In addition, there are higher expectations regarding support, quality, and technology, and many customers are looking for single suppliers and partnerships wherever possible.

Competitors. The most common changes cited by managers were a sizable amount of consolidations and mergers. Now there are fewer, but larger competitors. Many competitors are using global sourcing and global suppliers and can make deep price cuts to take market share.

Suppliers. The most common changes cited by managers were that fewer choices exist due to business failures and consolidations. Many suppliers are looking for long-term partnerships and continue to pass logistics costs on to customers, increasing the cost of raw materials and supplies.

The Company Itself. The most common changes cited by managers were that their companies were becoming flatter and more team-based. In addition, they felt that it has become more difficult to serve their customers because of limited resources, and they experience fewer benefits and incentives for higher levels of performance.

Tools to Support Change

Responding to rapidly changing market dynamics is an ongoing challenge in organizations. The rate and speed of change continue to increase, and there's continual demand that tools be in place to take advantage of opportunities and problems that impact sustainability and survival. The emphasis here is on assessing risks and responding by removing obstacles that deter progress toward company objectives. Other tools are available as referenced in the Appendix.

Risk Assessment

The risk assessment should be completed as part of the objective planning process, during the early part of the business year. This assessment will bring visibility to the overall risks associated with the completion of a critical objective. The idea of this assessment is to look at the risk factors and determine the degree of risk for each of these factors and the overall risk potential. These risk factors can then be monitored periodically to ensure that problems are identified quickly and responses can be initiated immediately.

When you're assessing the risk factors, consider using a chart similar to the one in Exhibit 7-1 that can accompany the functional plans and objectives.

Let's say that a critical objective for the Operations Group is to specify on-time parts delivery to support production and customer shipping requirements. It's critical for them to secure the parts at a reasonable price, when needed to meet production schedules. This objective ties into the company business plan for increased customer satisfaction and customer response. Using this chart can help to assess, monitor, and respond to risk factors. A risk potential of 3 or more should be monitored on a monthly basis.

Risk Factor	A. Likelihood of Risk: 1–5	B. Degree of Risk: 1–5	Risk Potential A x B	Method of Overcoming
Price Fluctuations —will impact margins				Lock in pricing for 6–12 months
Meet Production Demands— missed schedule creates customer issues				Impose late penalties Identify second source

Exhibit 7-1. Figuring risk potential

"WHAT IF" SCENARIOS   SMART

The main purpose of "what if" scenarios is to identify the potential risks and events that could go wrong and derail a major objective or the entire plan. These "what if" scenarios should be used with a risk assessment. This can be accomplished by placing the "what   MANAGING if" selections into the risk factor category and adding (potential) in parenthesis. When discussing the possible outcomes of these "what if" scenarios, this can be added to the methods of overcoming them.

Force Field Analysis

The work of Dr. Kurt Lewin was discussed in Chapter 5 as it related to making a culture shift. The model presented applies directly to any change process that requires a structured approach and predictable outcomes. A complementary tool called the Force Field Analysis was also developed by Dr. Lewin. This tool provides a structured way to look at the forces that drive the change forward and the forces that restrain the change from happening. The center line represents the equilibrium or current situation in which these forces are applied. This equilibrium is also the baseline measurement for going forward and assessing progress toward the change or improvement goal. Exhibit 7-2 shows a model for developing a force field diagram. Exhibit 7-3 shows a diagram for analyzing forces for and against increasing on-time deliveries.

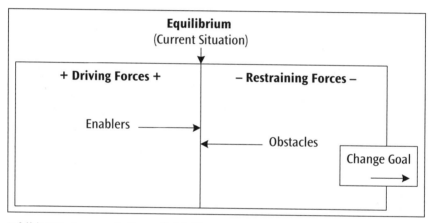

Exhibit 7-2. A generic force field diagram

The value of the Force Field Analysis is the action planning that's initiated as a result of the identification of the driving and restraining forces. The goal is to develop recommendations and supporting actions designed to strengthen the driving forces and remove the restraining forces.

Turnaround Situations

The American economy has been faced with several downturns, including bona fide recessions where there was decline in the Gross Domestic Product (GDP) for at least two consecutive quarters. These negative impacts are felt on employment, industrial production, real income, and wholesale/retail sales. The effects of these poor economic conditions have devastated businesses, irrespective of size. The ripple effects in

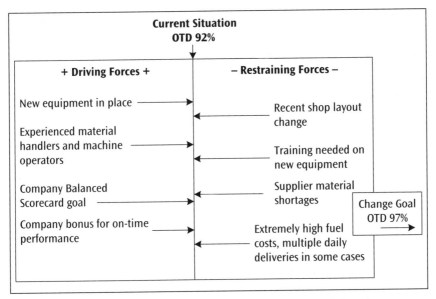

Exhibit 7-3. Force Field Analysis for improving on-time deliveries

industries such as the automotive industry have placed suppliers at the risk of going out of business. Even government bailout help is only a temporary solution. Many of these companies find themselves in turn-around situations in which immediate action is required. Strategies and contingency plans can be focused on these key areas for immediate improvements. Cost-cutting may be effective if the company has high direct labor costs or high fixed expenses that can be trimmed for quick bottom-line results. Another approach is to target these efforts toward increasing revenues by expanding products and services into new geographies or markets. New product development can help by penetrating existing markets or reaching into new markets. Asset reduction is also a method of cost reduction, especially if other cost-cutting methods have been exhausted. We will discuss outsourcing as a contingency approach later in this chapter. It may be necessary to use a combined approach, mixing all of the above techniques.

Activating Contingency Plans

The only constant we can depend on is change. A mindset of flexibility is a requirement if objectives are to be achieved. Dealing with business change is not always responding to adverse conditions, but might mean responding to an upside change, such as a large, unexpected order or the addition of a profitable customer from a competitor. In any event, contingency plans must be activated to remedy a problem or to seize an opportunity.

Internal SCAN

A planning and action tool called the SCAN is designed to outline a situation that may be a problem and then to identify the challenges, analyze, and navigate to a successful result. This may be a way to develop contingency plans during the business year.

Situation. Understanding the business situation is the first step in determining what challenges must be addressed for the business to have a successful year and meet its objectives and plans. One way to decide on functions and/or areas that need attention is to look for cues in the environment. These cues may signal that improvements are required during the business year, some of which are unforeseen. Cues such as loss of a key customer, lower margins, and spikes in costs and expenses will need immediate attention.

In defining the situation, write a brief paragraph or series of bullet points describing how things actually are today. The current situation should be written as a description rather than an evaluation and should isolate a major challenge that needs to be addressed.

Challenge. The challenge selected in the current situation description is then crafted into a problem statement that details what's happening today in terms of specific issues, problems, and concerns. When scoping out the challenge, discuss what is or isn't happening and the impact on the business.

Analyze. Once the problem statement is written and clarity around the challenge has been established, apply the tools we present in the Appendix. Tools such as cause-and-effect Analysis and Pareto charts can identify the root cause and lead to a determination of a solution.

Navigation. Navigation is the completion of an action plan and the implementation of the action steps designed to solve the problem and meet the challenge identified as critical to the success of the company.

> ### ENVIRONMENTAL SCAN
>
> **TOOLS**
>
> As a regular management practice, it's advisable to scan the external environment to identify changes that might have an impact on your business. Examples of this include economic, technological, and regulatory changes that require a response, both for the short and long term. Scanning involves paying attention to the signals and trends and keeping abreast of industry developments. This will require the periodic review of trade journals and the Internet. It will trigger discussions of this information with colleagues and your team. This can lead to creative brainstorming and identification of negative or positive trends that will affect business performance.
>
> A consumer products company that learned about impending laws in California was able to respond to environmental protection legislation that would ban gas-powered lawn equipment in the next few years. They were able to shift some of the new product development from gas- to electric-powered products.

Cost Management versus Cost Reduction Programs

One of the approaches to adjusting to change and adversity is to focus on the costs of the organization with an eye toward reducing costs and expenses where possible. Many companies start by looking for any and all opportunities to cut costs, which is the most logical approach. The caution here is that cost reduction may create situations where the reductions may have a negative impact on service to the customer. A classic example is the reduction of staff as one of the first areas of investigation in a situation where costs are out of control. One company used a voluntary resignation program and lost key personnel in several areas that had a major negative impact on customer perception and satisfaction levels.

Outsourcing

Outsourcing may be a viable option—using a third party to manage functions and assets currently performed inside the company. There are several reasons for considering outsourcing, which may include:

- Reduce or control operating expenses.
- Compensate for lack of internal resources.
- Cash infusion.
- Free up capital funds.

When looking for outsourcing opportunities, the areas to pay particular attention to that may lead to a decision are:

- The business—looking for functions and assets inconsistent with the core business objectives and that have consistently poor performance and productivity results.
- Cost—looking for situations where costs may be high relative to the market and where capital can be better spent elsewhere in the company.
- Technology—looking for areas where the technology is rapidly changing and may be too expensive to update.
- Customer—looking for situations where customers are dissatisfied with products or services and their demands are increasing and becoming more complex to serve.
- Environment—looking for product and service providers who are readily available and can deliver cost, quality, and speed to customers.

The benefits of outsourcing include reduction of capital investments, potential cash infusion, and opportunities to reduce costs and staffing. Some of the risks associated with outsourcing include loss of control of the resources, customer dissatisfaction, and loss of in-house expertise.

Criteria for Making an Outsourcing Decision. The question to answer is, what are the best opportunities for outsourcing? Exhibit 7-4 shows a way to analyze alternatives. This approach can work for functional as well as asset outsourcing considerations.

Getting Started with Outsourcing Opportunities. The most effective way to gear up for outsourcing is to form a small team of cross-functional representatives who can serve as the planning and execution committee. The purpose of this team is to evaluate the current business environment and select candidates for outsourcing. This team will also develop the criteria for selection, evaluation, and decision making. In addition, the team must have guidelines on how to deal with people issues, especially if job loss is imminent.

Cost Management: Dealing with People Issues

In the event of a cost reduction situation that involves reassignments, furloughs, and layoffs, it's critical that the company make these deci-

Decision Criteria	Outsource	Remain In-House
Customer View of the Function	Customers are most concerned with outputs, not process. If capabilities are available in the market from qualified suppliers, it may make sense to outsource.	The function requires specialized capabilities for which there are no qualified suppliers.
Technology	The technology is either mature and stable or dynamic and changing at a rapid rate, and it's not cost effective to adapt.	The possession of technology represents a clear competitive advantage.
Performance	Significant investment is required to achieve the performance level expected by customers.	Performance is at or can be elevated to meet customer expectations.
Long-Term View	There's an opportunity to exit the function in the near future.	Long-term commitment exists to maintain the function and financial and human resources are available.

Exhibit 7-4. Deciding to outsource or not

sions objectively and in an unbiased fashion to avoid legal challenges and their consequences. The planning process should involve a review of the functional plans and budgets, which includes the staffing forecast. Examples of this format are shown in Chapter 3 with respect to human resource planning. When business performance falls below expectations, in terms of revenues and profitability, the functional staffing requirements should be reviewed to determine what work is unnecessary in the current business environment. Decisions regarding a reduction in personnel should be made according to performance, years of service, and skills requirements for the future. A partial solution to this situation may be to initiate a hiring freeze and allow employee attrition to reduce staffing to required levels. Many companies will try to reassign personnel rather than a staff reduction. When this isn't possible, extending benefits and providing some form of outplacement support can help to retain the goodwill of the workforce.

Being Proactive: Business Tune-Ups

A proactive approach to contingency planning is to conduct annual business tune-ups designed to uncover and identify situations that can be improved in the business. By asking the right questions, issues that need attention will surface. The subsequent actions can be prioritized as short- or long-term solutions.

TUNE-UP AREAS AND QUESTIONS

Rate each question: 1 = not at all; 2 = Minimally; 3 = Somewhat; 4 = Mostly; 5 = Completely

TOOLS

Planning
- How well is the current business plan being implemented? _____

- How effective is the plan review process, especially with regard to making adjustments? _____

Growth Rate
- How well does the growth rate of sales compare to expectations?_____
- Have margin rates kept pace with changes in the marketplace? _____

Product and Service Capabilities
- How well does the company understand how products and services fit into customer needs? _____
- How well does the company differentiate its products/services from those of competitors? _____

Cost Control
- Does the company concentrate on ways to control costs? _____
- How well does the measurement system contribute to cost control efforts? _____

Productivity and Quality
- Has the company kept pace with state-of-the-art quality management techniques? _____
- How well has the company upgraded its information technology capability? _____

Case Example: Making Adjustments

A well-established engineering company was recently hit hard by the economic downturn. One of its major projects, a five-star hotel and conference center, lost an important investor and the project completion was in jeopardy. The business owner decided to conduct a mid-year review of the business plan and look for opportunities to make adjustments that would lead the business to a successful yearly performance.

Identify Business Strengths. The real strengths of this business are that it has been in business for 23 years and has built a reputation with clients and suppliers that will pay dividends in the future. The geography has growth opportunities. The 30 or so employees of the company are assets and can be tapped to help to find ways to improve the business. A major goal would be to first get their arms around the business, meet with managerial and professional employees, and engage them in the effort of making the business more competitive in the future. This, combined with some tools in place, would be very powerful.

Identify Business Opportunities. After reviewing the day-to-day management processes and systems, there are gaps in use of customer and financial information, the workforce is not being used to its fullest capability, and there is a lack of documented plans to use as measurements. A list of focus areas includes, but is not limited to, the following:

- **Identify Sources of Funding.** Immediately locate a source for a $14 million construction loan. Initiate contact with commercial bankers immediately.
- **Marketing, Business Development, and Sales Plan.** Build a customer file, create a prospect file, and conduct a quick-hitting marketing program to communicate with customers and prospects (option: identify a service). Eliminate peaks and valleys.
- **Financial Management.** Create a quarterly P&L, review credit, collections, and receivables recent history, and look for opportunities to tighten up the process. Communicate financial performance on a quarterly basis.

- **Full Use of Manpower Capabilities.** Find opportunities to fully use staff resources through short-term consulting projects. Use websites such as www.sologig.com to locate opportunities.
- **Strategic Management and Business Plan.** Uncover opportunities to expand services and geographies to drive new business. This will be coupled with the marketing and sales plan.
- **Efficiency.** Use Lean Operations Techniques to find ways to eliminate waste by reducing cost and non-value-added activities.
- **Exit Strategy.** Make the business viable to a third party.

PLANNING FOR CONTINGENCIES

For each focus area below, you will find the business objectives and the action planning required to successfully achieve these objectives.

PLANNING

Business Objectives

- Communicate to past, current, and prospective customers, looking for the "sweet spot" of need meeting service capability.
- Create an action plan to close business—eliminate peaks and valleys in orders and client work.

Action Planning

- Build a customer file, create a prospect file, and conduct a quick-hitting marketing program to communicate with customers and prospects. Adding to this would be to let them know of a new service that's available.

FINANCIAL MANAGEMENT

Business Objectives

- Produce real-time financial data to support decision making and provide tools to demonstrate how the business is performing.
- Tighten up receivables, credit, and collection to reduce time accounts receivables are outstanding.

Action Planning

- Create P&L, customer receivables analysis, analyze balance sheet, look for ways to reduce tax exposures, and look for tax relief in a slower business year.

FULL USE OF MANPOWER CAPABILITIES

Business Objectives

- Manage downtime during and between projects.
- Look for ways to immediately use and deploy professional staff and talents.

Action Planning

- Identify talent and consulting skills on staff.
- Use Internet and technical consulting groups to identify opportunities to use the staff.

STRATEGIC MANAGEMENT AND BUSINESS PLAN

Business Objective

- Uncover opportunities to expand services and geographies to drive new business.

Action Planning

- Complete the strategic marketing matrix to identify specifically where to build the business in both existing and new markets, with an eye on new services that complement current portfolio.

EFFICIENCY

Business Objective

- Eliminate waste and non-value-added work. Become more efficient in everything we do.

Action Planning

- Use Lean Operations Techniques and awareness training to emphasize continuous improvement in both safety and efficiency with the elimination of waste and non-value-added activities.

EXIT STRATEGY

Business Objective

- Identify an exit strategy to leave the business.

Action Planning

- Make the business attractive. Involve more people in day-to-day operations. Transition from owner-centered to business-centered operations.

CURRENCY FLUCTUATIONS

A key factor in operating in export markets is the currency exchange rate movements. The nature of the worldwide currency markets means that predicting the future is almost impossible. There are many factors that affect the currency exchange rates from all around the globe, but we are still bound by supply and demand affecting the rates. Interest rates in foreign countries will also impact how business is conducted. It makes sense to plan and monitor currency and interest rates in a global business environment and identify this situation in a risk assessment so that contingency plans can be created.

Increasing Sales Productivity

The overall objective is to decrease sales and marketing costs, increase revenue, and improve bottom-line performance through higher-quality outside sales execution. In addition, it's important to implement a structure for continuous improvement through focus, discipline, and a coaching process built on accountability.

Fine-Tune the Selling Process

- Begin with the prospect or customer. Spend more time trying to understand their world. *Act like an "insider."* Use the key skills of research and planning.
- Create the opportunity to interact. *Establish credibility and trust.* Use your experience, knowledge, and contacts to engage the prospect/customer. Use the key skill of customer engagement.
- Be prepared to ask questions. *Identify specific needs/opportunities* that you can take advantage of using existing or new products. Use the key skills of listening to the customer and confirming their wants and needs.
- *Build a strong business case/proposal* that presents the financial and long-term advantages of working with your company. Use your internal team of sales, product management, engineering, and finance to present the best thinking of the company. Use the key skill of preparing a successful proposal.
- *Present your case to the prospect or customer.* Listen carefully for reactions and opportunities and ways to enable collaboration. Use the key skills of presentation and collaboration.
- *Work out terms collaboratively.* Get commitment. Turn intent into a contract. Use the key skills of negotiation and reaching agreement.
- *Start over.* Recycle the method for existing and new accounts.

Optimize Selling and Service Time

Often customer accounts aren't viewed as investments in time and money, and may get unnecessary attention based on their actual and potential sales volume.

Account Management. The major goals are to increase revenue, decrease costs, and enhance the customer experience with a focus on improved service and outside sales coverage within your existing account base. Ability to classify your customers in terms of their current sales and future potential can help to determine how to service these customers and where priorities should be placed. Set up a simple matrix in which you're matching the actual sales with the potential for add-on or up-selling. These accounts have low actual sales and low potential, and require little investment. They can be considered "take it or leave it" customers.

The accounts that have high potential and high actual sales are your top customers and demand attention. The accounts that have low actual sales but high potential are considered target accounts. Other considerations include low potential and high actual sales where you want to be service-oriented, but not necessarily in a business-building mode. The main purpose of this assessment is to evaluate the potential and actual sales performance of your accounts and determine how to prioritize account management.

Business Continuity Planning

As was stated in Chapter 1, many businesses don't plan for disasters that may cripple their ability to serve customers.

A disaster may be considered any condition that prevents you from performing your critical business functions in an acceptable time to serve your customers.

Business continuity plans identify potential impacts that threaten an organization and provide a framework for building effective response and recovery, if required. The planning begins at the strategic level by assessing, in advance, the potential impacts of a wide variety of sudden disruptions to the organization's ability to succeed. While terrorist attacks, fires, storms, and floods capture the headlines, a large portion of incidents go unreported. In managing any event, critical areas such as information management, facility management, and security should be considered as potential areas for disasters to occur.

Once the potential exposures are identified, the company-wide responses can be prepared in a disaster recovery plan. The overall goal of these plans is to prevent significant loss of operating capability and reduce the risk of danger to the staff.

Don't be trapped into thinking that these disasters can't happen to you. Integrate continuity planning into both strategic and business planning processes.

Manager's Checklist for Chapter 7

☑ Understand the changes occurring in your marketplace.

☑ Use the tools for managing risk and change.

☑ Use cost management tools such as outsourcing and business tune-ups.

☑ Apply SCAN techniques and proactive management to identify issues early.

☑ Consider using the techniques designed to increase sales productivity.

☑ Consider continuity planning as a way to respond to disasters.

Recycle Your Learning

The ability to learn quickly is the essence of applying learning to work-related situations and making use of planning and execution experiences. This involves learning from one planning period to the next and applying that learning to improve the performance of the business. In thinking about the importance of organizational learning, consider the following comment made by Arie de Geus, Dutch writer and author: "The only sustainable competitive advantage is the ability to learn faster than the competition." Your ability to adapt to change and learn from mistakes will give you many opportunities to sustain your business in the marketplace over time.

Creating a Learning Organization

A learning organization can be described as a company with the capacity to anticipate customer needs and respond to change rapidly and effectively. The characteristics of people in learning organizations include a strong desire to learn from every situation and to focus on reaching and exceeding their expected results. These people embody creative thinking and innovation and are open and honest about admitting mistakes.

As business becomes increasingly dynamic and complex, the successful organizations will be those that discover how to increase commitment and capacity to learn at all levels of the organization.

Foundation of a Learning Organization

Learning Is a Requirement for Success. Create an environment where learning is part of the business expectations. Employees should be expected to have a continuous learning mindset.

Measuring Learning Is a Requirement for Success. Learning must become part of the overall company strategy and then become part of its measurement system. Adding a learning component to a Balanced Scorecard is one way to emphasize and measure it. The commitment to learning can also be built into the performance and development system and become part of the annual review process. Each individual should have up to three learning goals for each business year, and this should be planned, documented, and clearly linked to better achievement of objectives and plans.

Creating Learning Opportunities Is a Requirement for Success. Many organizations provide in-house training opportunities for employees to upgrade and learn new skills. In some cases, specialized learning needs can be accommodated through the use of external seminars. The key to success is that each individual has a commitment to learning and has a mindset toward self-directed learning. The test of this commitment is that development plans are documented and completed.

Learning about the Customer Is a Requirement for Success. You must be learning as fast as your customer. Constant communication with your customer, customer satisfaction assessments, and focus groups can all provide opportunities for feedback and better understanding of customer thinking and priorities. The idea is to be able to think like your customer and anticipate needs in advance.

KEY TERM — **Self-directed learning** This is the ability of an individual to identify their learning needs and opportunities and to engage in fulfilling those through a variety of techniques. Methods of self-directed learning include self-instructional programs such as tutorials and electronic learning programs available on the Internet or via DVD. Internal and external workshops, seminars, and information exchanges also can fill individual learning needs when company programs aren't specialized enough. The most important aspects of self-directed learning are a recognition of the learning need, a commitment to learning, and a plan to activate the learning process.

How to Learn

Learning styles vary along with learning speed. It's valuable for each person to identify what their preferred learning styles are and to find ways to optimize their ability to learn. Three learning styles are visual, auditory, and tactile/kinesthetic. Visual learners prefer using images, pictures, colors, and maps to organize information and communicate with others. They can easily visualize objects, plans, and outcomes. They may also possess a good sense of direction and are comfortable using maps to get around. They also like drawing, scribbling, and doodling, especially with colors. The auditory style prefers listening to words and sounds, creating an image from them. They like to hear speakers and try to retain the information from the spoken word. Auditory learners are often music lovers. The third style, tactile/kinesthetic, prefers doing or getting involved in the learning situation. Taking notes on paper or at a computer will help with retention of information, as well as engaging in some form of movement.

If you know your preferred learning style (you may have more than one), you can optimize the use of that style, but you should be prepared to use a blend of styles to maximize your learning opportunities. You can complete one of several free online assessments. Just search for "free learning styles assessments" in your Internet browser.

Rapid Learning Model

Rapid learning requires a structured approach in which the learner first creates recognition of the learning need. This can be achieved by identifying the specific learning area or competency and defining what excellence is or what the best practices are. This should be followed by a self-assessment of individual competence, uncovering both strengths and learning needs. To improve on a learning need, content such as reading material, DVDs, or other media should be identified to close the gap.

Knowledge Management

A gap in organizations today is the ability to share information and knowledge gained in day-to-day business operations. This is at the core of using rapid learning to gain competitive advantage. Obstacles that stand in the way of this sharing of knowledge include multiple locations and the organization structure itself. The traditional, functional, or hierarchical structures can create a mentality of sub-optimization in which the goal is to focus on only the work at hand and to achieve functional plans at all costs. Individual performance, rather than team performance, is rewarded in the same way. Some companies use a matrix structure that's more integrated and mixes functional structure with project teams and other types of multifunctional teams. This type of structure encourages more information sharing because of joint goals and objectives.

A technique being used to accelerate the sharing of learning is called knowledge management. In this context, knowledge management is considered the full use of information and data, in conjunction with the full use of skills and capabilities of the workforce to go beyond the expected results.

Knowledge is power. By the same token, unused knowledge is the loss of power. Companies that effectively use knowledge management are able to transfer information quickly and accurately throughout the organization. This includes sharing information within and between groups. These companies can generate ideas quickly in a creative process, but can also turn those ideas into innovative solutions to customer needs and problems. In addition, they're able to anticipate needs and respond to rapid change.

Applied Learning

The most powerful method of learning is in the organizational classroom where actual work issues and problems are discussed. Several opportunities exist for both individual and group learning. I've listed a few of the best ways to learn faster than your competition.

Best Practices

A best practice is an idea, process, or technique that's proven to be more effective at delivering a particular outcome and has a track record of effectiveness. Simple, repeatable processes are especially important for companies that are trying to grow from a small to a medium-sized business. Best practices are the processes of developing and following a standard way of

> **Action learning** Action learning is a methodology that brings
> people together to work on actual business issues in a forum
> that emphasizes analysis and learning to solve day-to-day busi-
> ness problems. The groups may vary in size and organization   **KEY TERM**
> level and be teamed up in small groups to identify, prioritize, and solve
> problems chosen by company leaders. The forums are most successful
> when they use a structured agenda and a facilitator. Often problem-solving
> tools are introduced during the forum and are immediately applied to the
> problem-solving challenges of the small teams. The results of the forum can
> provide a springboard into the next phase of implementation.

doing things that can eliminate duplication and waste while increasing speed of delivery of the work products and outputs. The goal of best practices identification is to develop a benchmark of excellence that should be a world-class standard that can provide a target for the future.

After you've decided the areas in which you want to find best practice benchmarks (review sidebar in Chapter 1: What Should Be Benchmarked?, on page 11), the next step is to identify best practice sources that exhibit outstanding performance in your areas of interest. You can easily find these companies by conducting online searches, contacting state and national Quality and Productivity Centers, and using trade publications and associations. Once you've identified the key area and source of best practices, often company websites will offer case studies and resource information. Past Malcolm Baldrige Award winners offer summaries of how they achieved excellence in their organizations. Many of the companies that have been identified as best practice organizations are receptive to visits to learn more about their achievements and approaches to business process improvement and other breakthroughs. Obviously there will be a limit on information shared, but it can be a good start.

Lessons Learned Analysis

The Lessons Learned Analysis seeks the information and knowledge gained from analyzing both positive and negative experiences of a project, program, or major objective. The purpose of this exercise is to use the findings to improve performance. It should become a discipline for every company manager to conduct a post-assessment of their major efforts at the end of a project or end of the business year.

Lessons Learned Format

Conducting a Lessons Learned Analysis involves asking questions about the performance and results of the project, program, or major objectives. You want to look at both the process and the outcomes with a goal of learning the strengths and improvement areas going forward, applying this learning to future plans. The questions should be grouped into quantitative and qualitative sections and the data generated should be shared among all the team members.

Sample Lessons Learned Format

Use the templates in Exhibits 8-1 through 8-3 to conduct a Lessons Learned debriefing with your team.

Section 1. Project/Quantitative Results

Category	Performance Actual vs. Planned	Learning
Quantity: How well were the targets/outputs achieved?		
Quality: How well were the targets for reducing defects, scrap, and waste met?		
Timeliness: Were the objectives delivered on time? Were the milestones met?		
Cost: Did the final results meet the financial targets, budget, or expense limits?		

Exhibit 8-1. Lessons Learned template, part 1

Section 2. Project/Qualitative Results

Category	Assessment	Learning
Internal Customer Feedback		
External Customer Feedback (refer to questionnaire on the next page)		
Timeliness: Were the objectives delivered on time? Were the milestones met?		
Leadership Effectiveness: How effective was the team leader in planning, guiding, and motivating the team?		

Exhibit 8-2. Lessons Learned template, part 2

Section 3. Processes, Procedures, and Structure

Category	Learning and Adjustments
Procedures: How did the procedures help or hinder the results achieved?	
Processes: How well did the supporting processes contribute to the objectives?	
Structure: How well did the structure of the team help to deliver the results?	

Exhibit 8-3. Lessons Learned template, part 3

OBTAINING EXTERNAL CUSTOMER FEEDBACK: SHORT QUESTIONNAIRE

TOOLS

Products and Services. How well did the products and services conform to the agreed-on specifications? How reliable were the products and services?

Customer Service. How easy is it for the customer to do business with you regarding placing orders, changing orders, quotation turnaround times, invoice accuracy, and deliveries?

Problem Solving. How quickly were problems responded to and was the problem resolved satisfactorily every time?

Overall Performance. Compared to other suppliers, was your performance better, equal to, or worse? Why?

SMART

THE SPEED OF YOUR LEARNING

MANAGING

Learning speed can be considered the rate at which individuals and organizations acquire knowledge, assimilate that knowledge, and apply it to the work environment. There are many ways to accelerate learning in today's organizations and the information age. Companies are using electronic learning to make the learning process more convenient to employees. In these situations, presentations and learning modules are delivered to the desktop computer via internal networks through the Internet. This learning is self-paced and often has checks for understanding and quizzes to ensure the individual has acquired and can use the information.

Two Examples

New Product Development

An industrial products manufacturer recently completed a new product development project and conducted a Lessons Learned Analysis with its project teams and functional support groups to determine areas for improvement. The goal was to learn what could be immediately applied to the next generation of product development scheduled for the next business year. They grouped their learning areas into five categories: recurring problems related to critical performance dimensions, crucial activities and tasks, cross-functional coordination, development speed, and decision making. A survey was designed to ask questions in each category and the project team members and support personnel completed the questionnaire. Results were tabulated and reviewed in a roundtable discussion to further enhance the learning process.

Lessons Learned

The learning derived from the survey and discussion of the results highlighted several opportunities for immediate improvements, including eliminating late-feature inductions through a design freeze guideline, more upstream involvement from the support groups through the establishment of a formal multifunctional team structure and commitments, early role clarification, and better decision-making processes through a set of team operating procedures and team norms.

Insights for Future Project Teams

- Build the team climate and culture. Establish team norms for early identification of problems, rather than waiting and creating bigger problems down the road.
- Create a risk assessment for new technology and new features. Build adequate time and contingencies into the schedule.
- Conduct in-depth supplier audits to ensure capabilities and commitments are met.
- Consider using project leads for major subprojects. This will provide opportunities for the project manager to delegate more.
- Show some reluctance to move project team members between ongoing projects. This can create gaps at critical times during the product development cycle.

Operations

A service department of a major parts distributor conducted a customer satisfaction survey and identified three key areas for improving customer service. Since the service department was primarily a telephone response team, customers wanted less waiting time and wanted to speak to a representative more quickly than navigating through a long series of

TRICKS OF THE TRADE

PUTS AND CALLS

An action learning technique called Puts and Calls can be used as an exercise in any forum in which information is shared, especially when problem solving is occurring. Use a flip chart or a white board. A topic is selected with the title created as the header on the flip chart or white board. For example, discussing failure mode and effects analysis may be an important topic for information sharing and learning.

A center line is drawn on the flip chart or white board, with Puts on one side and Calls on the other side. The terms are in the same context as the stock market. A Call is a request for information and a Put is an offer of information on the topic. Participants can write their puts and calls on sticky notes along with their names and post them on the appropriate sides of the board.

During the meeting breaks, participants can study the postings and make contact with other participants to give or receive the information. It's an informal way to share learning needs and expertise.

prompts and ending up on hold. In addition, they wanted to know that their requests had been processed immediately. After the improvements were put in place, a second survey was conducted a year later. Although the satisfaction levels improved in most areas, some customers still complained about lack of responsiveness. The service manager decided to conduct a Lessons Learned Analysis with the service department, warehouse, and shipping departments. They met in a roundtable format, first reviewing the customer survey quantitative results and then reviewing the customer comments in terms of themes.

Lessons Learned

Although the service department had specific metrics for improvement, the warehouse and shipping departments tracked their response times but had no improvement goals. In fact their average order fill time was more than three days, with an additional one to two days for shipping.

The warehouse and shipping departments received little customer feedback and did not have a very clear idea of what they should be working on to improve. An action item was developed to review, track, and monitor order fulfillment and shipping rates. This was followed by the identification of industry best practices to establish improvement targets.

The biggest lesson learned was that in this service chain, the front end can be considered world-class, but the other links must deliver cost, quality, and speed in the same manner to best serve their customer.

GE Workout

The GE (General Electric) Workout was developed in the late 1980s as a way to bring small groups of managers, employees, and cross-functional membership together to address important business issues. The idea behind the formation of these groups is that those closest to the work know it best. When participation is combined with a process that facilitates the identification of key business issues in a focused, action-oriented workshop, the results can be powerful.

Workout Roles

The sponsor is a senior manager who has the responsibility for all levels of departments and employees involved in the workout sessions. This is a mandatory role.

- The *champion* is a representative of the sponsor who attends the workout sessions and is responsible for planning and follow-up.
- The *facilitator* is a person who has experience with the workout process and is responsible for the session design, logistics, and facilitation of the agenda.
- The *team leaders* are responsible for briefing and preparing their employees for participation in the workout sessions.
- The *team members* are the participants in the workout sessions and are responsible for analyzing and developing the recommendations to solve the business issues at hand.

How the Workout Works

The overall goal of the GE Workout is to form small groups of managers, supervisors, team leaders, and employees to address critical business issues. These groups may be cross-functional and/or cross-level, depending on their closeness to the problem or challenge at hand. The group, using the Workout Roles, evaluates the business issue and presents its recommendations to senior leaders in a town meeting format. The group then makes a go/no-go decision about moving forward.

Crafting Your Own Workout

Using the GE Workout guidelines, you can form your own workout process by following the checklist and suggestions on the next page.

Your GE Workout Checklist

❑ Identify business issues that can best be addressed by a small, multiple-level problem-solving team. You may want to identify a few issues and give the workout team the opportunity to prioritize them during the session.

❑ Select the workout participants using the team roles for sponsor, champion, facilitator, and team members. You can create team selection criteria so that you enlist the support of those closest to the action.

❑ Build a workout agenda and meeting plan. You can use a one- or two-day format for meeting components such as sponsor kickoff, objectives, presentation of the business issues to be addressed, topic prioritization, and review of your problem-solving methodology. This should be followed by group analysis and presentations.

❑ Conduct a town meeting with the workout team and senior leaders to review the recommendations and make a go/no-go decision on whether to move ahead with the team recommendations.

After a few pilot workout sessions, a decision can be made about the continued use of the workout as a method to address key business problems.

Use a payoff matrix similar to the one shown in Exhibit 8-4 as a business issue selection tool to figure out which issues to address.

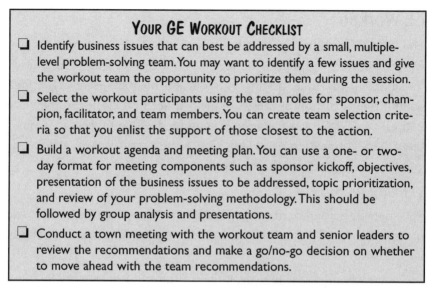

Exhibit 8-4. A payoff matrix

Team Action Planning

The Team Action Planning format is another way to bring groups together to engage in problem solving around key business issues. Using this format can add structure and help to reach the deliverables in a shorter time.

Task

The goal of the Team Action Planning is to provide a forum for work teams to develop specific actions designed to improve the regional/systemic issues identified by the leadership team. The specific objective is to develop action plans that can be immediately implemented and will have a positive impact on the productivity of the business unit or department.

Process

Part 1. Scoping the Problem

Method: Major Issue (use Worksheet 1)

A. For the major issue selected, describe the Current Situation. This is a brief paragraph or series of bullet points describing how things actually are today. The current situation is a problem statement and should describe rather than evaluate.

B. Next, the team should describe the Desired Future. This will be the vision of the future, the next 12 to 18 months, describing what success would look like.

C. Finally, the team should brainstorm recommendations that will help reach the desired future. Your purpose here is to come up with a list of about 10 possible recommendations. Don't worry at this point if each recommendation is suitable for a team to work on. A broad list will serve as a point of departure for action planning.

WORKSHEET 1. PROBLEM IDENTIFICATION

1. Identify the major problem, issue, or challenge.

2. Describe the current situation.

3. Describe the desired future.

4. Brainstorm: Recommendations/actions that will move you toward the desired future.

Part 2. Creating an Action Plan

Method: Use Worksheet 2

Once you've brainstormed recommendations, for each issue selected you can begin to complete action plans required to make the changes. The plan should be implemented within the next 30 days and the solution will make an impact on the business.

Action Steps Outline is an implementation approach to achieving the desired future. For each recommendation, identify 5 to 10 action steps that will be taken to implement the recommendation. Use the provided worksheets, one per recommendation. Action steps should be specific. "Who" refers to someone who will take responsibility for the action and "When" refers to the due date.

In working on the task and action steps:

- The required expertise should be identified to solve the problem
- The likelihood that a change will make a difference and is feasible should be determined
- The plan should be actionable within 1 to 3 months
- Identify the "customer" or responsible executive
  (Include steps to achieve approval, funding, etc.)

WORKSHEET 2. ACTION STEPS

Major Issue to Be Addressed:

Selected Recommendation:

Action Plan

Action Steps	Who	When

Leadership Through Learning

The success of an organization largely depends on the effectiveness of its leaders to provide the direction and inspiration to its workforce. The only way that a leader can fulfill this role is to become a continuous learner and to use this learning to increase the effectiveness of the organization. The focus of this learning is related to customers, markets, and competition, and is best used when cascaded through the organization. Making use of the communication system described in Chapter 5 is one good choice of a vehicle for successfully accomplishing this goal. In addition, company leaders should be involved in teaching and coaching their key managers and modeling expected behaviors and cultural norms.

TEACHABLE MOMENT

The teachable moment is a time at which a person is likely to be receptive to learn or particularly responsive to being taught something. This is an opportunity that a manager can take advantage of when coaching and developing people. Teachable moments can occur at any time, especially in adverse or difficult situations. One method of delivering the teachable message is to use a short Lessons Learned approach in which you are processing the learning in terms of what went well and what can be improved. This can be done in a group setting or in a one-on-one coaching session.

Technical Leadership and Execution

Use this assessment tool to identify and evaluate your competencies in leadership and execution, as two key areas in planning for results. For those areas in which you lack competence, you then have information on areas of improvement. Use this scale: 5 = Strongly Agree; 4 = Agree; 3 = Not Sure; 2 = Disagree; 1 = Strongly Disagree. Note that the items that receive 3 or less should become learning and improvement opportunities for the next 6 to 12 months.

---

1. Demonstrates technical knowledge necessary to lead the team _____
2. Demonstrates technical knowledge necessary to lead projects and programs _____
3. Introduces new methods for addressing technical problems _____
4. Coaches team in use of these new methods _____
5. Translates business implications of technical issues and processes the learning _____
6. Prioritizes action items based on technical and business implications
   _____
7. Sets aggressive, but realistic goals (technical, schedule, budget) _____

8. Demonstrates product/service development and processes knowledge _____
9. Demonstrates knowledge and proactively addresses multi-disciplinary and interdepartmental concerns _____

Manager's Checklist for Chapter 8

☑ Understand the elements of a learning organization.

☑ Use the tips on how to increase learning speed.

☑ Use action learning techniques such as the GE Workout.

☑ Create a discipline for using a Lessons Learned Analysis after each project completion.

☑ Increase individual learning by emphasizing self-directed learning.

☑ Evaluate your technical leadership and execution skills.

Tips and Traps to Avoid

No matter how carefully a plan is prepared and executed, something can and will go wrong. Paraphrasing the words of Robert Burns in his poem, "To a Mouse," "The best-laid plans of mice and men often go wrong." We have discussed ways of planning for change and developing contingency plans to deal with adversity. There are additional considerations to ponder at the beginning of the planning process and some traps to avoid in preparing and executing your plan. These tips and traps to avoid will help you make good use of lessons learned by others as they conduct post-project analyses on the results of their planning efforts.

Planning Tips

As you set aside time to begin your planning process, keep in mind some basic planning tips to guide your thinking.

1. Planning takes a commitment of time and energy. If you lack the attention to detail, find an individual to help you complete this work. Delegate the various components that require research and written summaries. It may be advantageous to find an outside contractor to complete the detailed planning, especially if a business plan document is required for sources of funding. The quality of these plans will often determine if a lender or investor will move forward on your request.

2. Use your network of other business contacts, suppliers, trade associations, chambers of commerce, and government agencies to get questions answered. These sources may be able to give you concrete examples of completed plans and guidance on what to include in your plans.

3. Think both long-term and short-term in creating your plans. Even though strategic planning has become more difficult with economic downturns and less predictable forecasts for customers, it's still the closest thing you have to a crystal ball. On the short-term side, focus on real-time monitoring and tracking of the plans and use contingency planning to respond to shortfalls and unplanned events.

4. Use quick decision making as a tool to take advantage of situations and opportunities as they present themselves. Conduct a Strengths, Weaknesses, Opportunities, and Threats (SWOT) Analysis to determine where you stand and what will need your attention in both the long and short term. This means both the positive and negative situations.

5. Take the responsibility for managing the plans yourself. You can delegate many aspects of the plan execution, but you must provide the oversight. If you're a functional manager, this means closely monitoring and tracking results so that you have early identification of issues and concerns. This will prevent blindsiding by a third-party analysis.

6. Budgets are your friend. It's impossible to run a business effectively without well-planned, accurate budget forecasts.

7. Consider working with local colleges or universities to attract business students for internships opportunities. Many companies have used MBA students to conduct research and make business recommendations in such key areas as market research, product development, and engineering. This is a partnership of mutual benefits, with the students gaining valuable business experience and the company receiving recommendations that may help them succeed in the marketplace.

8. Use the U.S. Small Business Administration, www.sba.gov, as a resource. There are many small business centers that can answer questions and provide guidance as you reach the final stages of your

plans. This type of real-world business insight can save much trial-and-error time.

9. Policies and procedures are necessary to provide guidance on acceptable management practices and to set boundaries.

10. Pay attention to culture. If there are legacy issues that could block contingency planning and planning for change, step in and become an architect of your culture. Identify and reinforce the behaviors required to drive your business strategies and plans.

ADDING VALUE

SMART

The concept of adding value has become a buzzword in business today. The real meaning of adding value has great significance in serving customers and growing a business. If it's applied correctly, adding value means providing product features and service com-   **MANAGING** ponents that enhance the value of what's received by the customer and that they're willing to pay for.

One example of this concept is to provide consultancy to your customers regarding the use of your products and services to help them achieve their business objectives and solve problems. Consultancy can be a natural extension of your product lines and services, and can create additional and new business opportunities. One business manager described it as helping customers fulfill their visions, not just their orders.

Encourage Creativity and Innovation

Organizations that find ways to stimulate creativity and innovation among their employees have a distinct advantage over their competition for the development of new products and services. Ideas for new products and services can come from anywhere. The traditional sources of research and development groups and customer focus groups should be modified to include opportunities for employees to engage in creative thinking and planning for new products and services. This is not a variation on the suggestion system, but a focus on bringing people together to brainstorm ideas and to develop innovative ways to bring new products and services to market ahead of the competition.

Creativity is the ability to generate many ideas to meet customer requirements. It's the ability to think outside the box. Innovation is the ability to translate these ideas into applications and to commercialize them into specific products and services that add value to the customer or solve

Not Invented Here Syndrome

Some organizations have the attitude that if something was not invented in their company, it's not worth using or applying. If this is the prevailing attitude, opportunities to take advantage of new ideas, best practices, or new ventures will be severely diminished. Breaking the Not Invented Here Syndrome requires strong intervention from senior leaders. They must send specific messages regarding being open to new ideas and practices, and frequently reinforce the message with their management teams.

customer problems. The skills required to engage in creative and innovative thinking are different and complementary. For example, creative thinkers are right-brain-oriented and have the ability to be imaginative and to see things in many different ways. They are not constrained by the past. The innovative thinkers are left-brain-oriented and have the ability to focus and select the best ideas. They have an implementation mentality and the ability to envision how a product or service will play in the marketplace. Bringing both types of thinkers together periodically can provide a wealth of new ideas and innovative suggestions on how to use them.

Planning for Technology Change

Planning for technology change is a way of life in organizations today. Create a master plan for technology, just as you would draw up a business plan, a budget, or a marketing plan. Design the plan so that it supports your business strategy and goals and use it as a guide for decision making. By having an overall plan, you can avoid wasting money on unnecessary purchases or quick fixes.

Implementing Technology Change. It's important to evaluate three critical business functions (as shown on the next page) prior to a technology implementation to ensure readiness for a successful transition. Many technology implementations fail to meet deadlines and deliver the enhancements that were used to gain approval for going forward. By using this analysis, risks can be avoided.

Process Planning. The assessment and planning process may be administered at any point during the project. It's recommended that this process be used to assess the initial project launch from a core team

---

CRITICAL BUSINESS FUNCTIONS REVIEW

Leadership

The leadership aspect of the technology implementation includes providing the direction and support required to meet ambitious schedules and deadlines.

Major Considerations

- Vision and supporting strategy that outline how the new technology will benefit the organization.
- Expectations for successful implementation and supporting management plans.
- Ongoing coaching and support for the implementation teams.

Operations

The operational aspect of the technology implementation includes procedures, processes, and policies that guide projects.

Major Considerations

- Processes and project plans that help to meet technology implementation plans.
- Work flow planning for new environment.
- Transition plans for reaching the future state, including performance standards and measurements.

People

The people aspects of the technology implementation include ensuring that there is a readiness for change and that people possess the necessary skills to productively use the technology.

Major Considerations

- Ongoing communication that addresses all concerns about the implementation status and benefits of the new technology.
- Ongoing training for both pre- and post-implementation.
- Application of incentives and rewards programs that recognize successful implementation and realization of the intended benefits of the new technology.

---

perspective, meaning that the team leaders can answer the assessment questions and get a "reality check" on the status of the launch. The optimum time that has proven to be effective is during the first 6 to 12 months of the project, because it can provide valuable data that can help the project get on track or stay on track, depending on individual situations in the organization.

Process Steps. The questions regarding the three critical business functions are formulated using the Question Planning Matrix. The target audience is selected, which might be a focus group, site implementation group, or other segment of the implementation. The question delivery method is decided (e-mail/online, focus groups, etc.).

The survey/assessment period is defined (one to two weeks) and data are collected and summarized for review by the core implementation team. Action items, including strengths and improvement areas, are identified. Action plans are developed as required, identifying who, what, and when scenarios. The action plans are monitored and progress reviewed regarding specific improvements and changes needed to make the project successful.

Positive Impacts
- Set clear expectations for the organization.
- Provide an opportunity to identify and remove project obstacles (Force Field Analysis).
- Establish training and communications priorities.
- Balance people needs with technical implementation goals.
- Motivate and reward the team members.
- Eliminate risks normally associated with project failures.
- Take the organization to a higher level of performance.

QUESTION PLANNING MATRIX

For each critical business function below, you will find the key questions and possible opportunities that correspond with these functions.

LEADERSHIP

Key Questions
- What is the vision for this project?
- How does it fit with the business strategy?
- How well are leaders and managers prepared to support the implementation?
- What are the tough issues that must be addressed currently?
- Are the businesses clear on the project goals, benefits, costs, and timelines?

Possible Opportunities
- Develop clear and concise communications around these critical messages.
- Conduct ongoing feedback sessions regarding project status.

- Conduct a Force Field Analysis to identify the driving and restraining forces impacting the project implementation. Plan to remove obstacles over time.

OPERATIONS

Key Questions

- What are the new processes to be implemented?
- How clearly is the operational/implementation plan communicated and understood?
- How will the technical modules be developed and implemented?
- Are business priorities and issues established?
- How will performance be measured?
- How well are processes aligned to add value to the customer?

Possible Opportunities

- Evaluate process maps and implementation plans.
- Use Lean Techniques for project management planning.
- Provide planning tools and formats to aid the implementation process.
- Provide change management awareness and training for all users.
- Establish metrics and milestones for measurement.

PEOPLE

Key Questions

- How clear are the communications to employees regarding the implementation and their responsibilities for the change?
- What new skills will employees need to be successful?
- What are the mindsets of the employees regarding the change—positive, neutral, or negative?
- What recognition events, techniques, etc., are planned to reinforce project successes?

Possible Opportunities

- Develop formal and informal communication networks to ensure that the key messages are received.
- Complete a skill assessment for pre- and post-implementation.
- Conduct workshops on how to deal with change designed to help gain commitment to the project implementation.
- Use *1001 Ways to Recognize Employees* by Bob Nelson for ongoing reinforcement.

Traps to Avoid

Regardless of the size of a business, there are mistakes that are common to many managers. Drawing attention to them may help avoid them during planning and execution. One major shortcoming is the lack of supporting plans from key areas of the business. In smaller businesses, these may be considered shared services or combined functional areas. In medium and large companies these will be the functional areas that drive the business. Subgroup plans may be missing and this will short-circuit execution. Even if plans exist, they may be weak and poorly prepared. Following are some classic traps to avoid during the planning and execution of your business plans.

1. **Lack of involvement:** Be wary of individuals who don't fully participate in the planning process. Cues such as missed meetings, lack of completed plans, and missed deadlines are early warning signals.

2. **Lack of commitment:** Commitment is what happens after the plans are completed. Be aware of individuals who become negative or critical of situations that require adjustments on their part and the part of the company. These individuals may be resistant to change and need intense coaching to get on track.

3. **Lack of detail or too much detail:** Plans that are too sketchy may lack the key ingredients for the subgroup planning process. Strategies should include high-level measurement and numbers, even if the subgroup's plans are expected to add specificity to the business plan. Plans that are steeped in graphs and heavy technical information may lose the key messages. Consider using summaries and adding the details in a reference file.

4. **Lack of communications or communication breakdowns:** Once plans are completed, the pace and frequency of communications drops off.

5. **Unrealistic projections and timelines:** Projections and deadlines that are unattainable or perceived as improbable are demotivating to those responsible for their execution. Challenging goals are critical to driving a business forward. Be wary of goals and objectives that cross the line into the demotivation zone.

6. **Lack of supporting functional plans:** Functional plans that don't reach their final state, with measurements and tracking information, will leave large gaps in helping to achieve the company objectives. Also they will make individual planning and creating performance standards difficult.

7. **Lack of operational reviews:** It's difficult to keep score in bowling if you can't see the pins. The same is true of operational performance. Conduct reviews at least on a quarterly basis and ask functions to conduct their own internal monthly reviews.

8. **Slow-moving response to problems:** It's not about the large companies versus small companies but more about the slow versus the nimble in responding to external market and internal issues.

9. **Shooting the messenger:** Be wary of individuals who don't accept corrective or unfavorable feedback, especially if it's intended to correct a problem. Individuals can become defensive when this type of feedback is presented. The style of the feedback is critical in setting the tone for mutual problem solving. The feedback giver can start the conversation by saying, "I have a concern. Can you tell more about ..."

10. **Miss the warning signs:** Early warning signs can go unnoticed or lack action at a point when problems can be solved with less difficulty and more speed. The key skill is to question everything and determine if a risk exists that must be addressed.

DATA DUMPS

A *data dump* is an attempt to share all available facts and figures. Data dumps will offer data rather than providing information that can be used for recommendations or conclusions. Data dumps often provide the answers to questions that may be unimportant and contain information of little relevance to the issues at hand.

To eliminate this problem, decide in advance in what format the data are to be presented to the planning teams. Use legibility standards for any visual presentations, such as PowerPoint. The data should be shared in advance of any discussions so that questions can be prepared in advance of a formal meeting. This can be a big time saver. Information presented that cannot be acted on or that is not useful in decision making doesn't add value to the planning process.

Ethics

In the past, the expectation of ethics and high standards was a given. The new millennium had spawned an era of corporate greed and unethical behavior that has crippled some businesses and created huge financial losses for stakeholders: customers, employees, and stockholders. What's missing for many organizations is an in-depth review of company policies and guidelines regarding employee codes of conduct and ethical behavior.

Company policy should be centered on a commitment to conduct oneself ethically and fairly in relation to customers, suppliers, competitors, and all other constituencies with whom you conduct business. In addition, policy should ensure that employees maintain the highest standards of business integrity in their relationships with the company and others outside the company. All employees must understand that even though they may be trying to do what is best for the company, they should not deal unfairly or take undue advantage of those with whom they are conducting business. The idea is to "play hard but fair." In publicly traded companies, there should also be ethical considerations preventing employees from making stock purchases or financial gains based on inside information.

Employees should be required to sign a Code of Conduct Statement on their date of employment and to reread and re-sign the statement annually to reinforce their commitments. Violators of this code should be subject to disciplinary action up to and including dismissal. Ensuring that ethical standards and behavior are institutionalized requires policy, role modeling, and consequences for violation of policy standards. Fair dealing means something a little different to each of us. Company policy and role modeling will help to focus personal codes of ethics on what is best for the company and its reputation in the industry.

INFLUENCES ON ETHICAL AND UNETHICAL BEHAVIOR

What influences one to make ethical decisions?

- Formal company policy
- An individual's personal code of behavior
- Ethical climate of the industry in which one competes or works
- Behavior of one's immediate manager
- Behavior of one's equals or peers

What influences one to make unethical decisions?

- Lack of company policy
- Personal financial needs
- Ethical climate of the industry in which one competes or works
- Behavior of one's immediate manager
- Behavior of one's equals or peers

Check In on Your Ethics

It's a question of ethics when you intend not to deal fairly and/or you break an ethical standard such as a code of conduct policy. You can be perceived as unethical or lacking integrity (ethical risk) when your personal or business code of ethics is less stringent than the observer's personal or business code of ethics. You can check yourself as you prepare to take action by looking for where the decision fits into this continuum.

- It helps you.
- There's no ground rule that says "Don't."
- There's a low risk of punishment if you get caught.
- It's socially acceptable and doesn't violate any socially accepted written standards.
- It doesn't violate generally accepted rights of others.
- It treats others' rights in the same way you would treat yours.
- Ask yourself, "Is this the right ethical decision?"

CONFLICT MANAGEMENT

TOOLS

Conflict is a natural occurrence during the planning process. Conflict is considered healthy when it's used to find common ground on a particular issue. The dynamic tension that exists in organizations can create conflict or a disagreement of opinion that will actually facilitate an effective solution or agreement.

Organizations that lack some conflict may risk becoming mediocre because they lack challenges to ideas and strategies. The most effective method of conflict management is to encourage a collaborative style in which disagreements are aired and discussed, with solutions including the interests of all parties. This helps to eliminate the competitive "my way or the highway" style of conflict resolution.

Your Planning Zone

The goal of every manager should be to reach a balance between planning and execution. If one is deficient in the planning stage, execution may occur more quickly, but the potential for errors or lack of contingencies may ultimately derail a plan. The other side of the coin is that when one is deficient in the execution, the best plans will have a limited chance for success. The expression "paralysis by analysis" applies here.

Plans can become lost in detail and momentum for execution is lost. Striking this balance is the key to planning for results.

One way to ensure that you have the right balance is to reach your "planning zone" in which your skill level matches your mental attitude and you're able to perform at your highest level. Many call this stage the mastery of a skill. Athletes often refer to themselves as being "in the zone" when they have that unique combination of preparation and actual performance on the field of play. You can reach your own level of the planning zone by thinking about how you plan and by following a simple mental model to stay in the zone.

Just as athletes engage in a process called results imaging, this same model works for developing a solid business focus. The process involves visualization of actual past events or thinking about participation in a future event. In addition, it's important to find a place to do your thinking that facilitates your ability to think and plan without normal distractions.

An example of results imaging was conducted by a nonprofit organization as a prelude to finalizing the plan for its annual fund drive. A team of volunteers was assembled for a planning meeting to identify the critical success factors that the organization had to address during the fund drive. The volunteers formed small teams and were given this assignment: "Think about a point in the future. It's 12 months from today.

> **SMART
> MANAGING**
>
> ## EMOTIONAL INTELLIGENCE
>
> Emotional Intelligence, as expressed by experts John Mayer and Peter Salovey, "is a type of social intelligence that involves the ability to monitor one's own and others' emotions, to discriminate among them, and to use the information to guide one's thinking and actions."
>
> Emotional Intelligence is focused on one's self-awareness and self-control and is useful in providing the emotional stability required in a changing, often chaotic business environment. Understanding your emotional triggers and using self-control are at the heart of exhibiting Emotional Intelligence.
>
> Mastery of these techniques can be motivational to yourself and others. In addition to this, Emotional Intelligence can help to enhance interpersonal relationships. Daniel Goldman has written several books on this subject and offers practical guidance on how to understand and use Emotional Intelligence techniques. This applies to both your business and personal interactions.

You're looking back on the recent fund drive, which was perhaps the most successful in history. List the actions, events, and other factors that would have led to such dramatic results."

The small teams captured their responses and presented them to the large group for feedback and discussion. The results were summarized and given to the fund drive planners as input for developing action plans and milestones they might have missed without conducting this exercise.

Manager's Checklist for Chapter 9

☑ Reflect back on your planning techniques and get a sense of how effective you are as a planner.

☑ Use the planning tips to improve your approach to planning.

☑ Review the planning traps and identify the current pitfalls in your planning process.

☑ Evaluate how the ethics guidelines apply to yourself and others who work in your organization.

☑ Strive to reach your planning zone.

Chapter 10

Personal Productivity

M uch success in planning and execution depends on personal productivity skills that help you organize and plan for implementation, improve time utilization, effectively present ideas, and increase your ability to delegate work to achieve ambitious goals. This chapter will provide a short review of these techniques on personal productivity, with suggestions on how to make improvements.

Getting Organized

Displaying some degree of organization skills is at the heart of personal productivity. We will discuss the enablers of personal productivity such as time management and meeting management shortly. Following are some quick suggestions regarding your ability to focus on sharpening organizational skills.

- **Be proactive.** When you're given a task or project work back from the end date. Immediately get your thinking around what needs to be done and who needs to be involved, even if the date is far out on your schedule.
- **Maximize your work space.** Look for opportunities to consolidate and organize your work space so that you are not wasting time constantly looking for materials that should be at your fingertips.

- **Develop a system to manage paper flow.** Although we're moving to an electronic, paperless society, we're far from it. Having a system that allows you to file and retrieve both electronic and paper documents is a survival technique. Limit the number of times you handle documents. File, take action, or discard unnecessary paper immediately.
- **Master the technology.** The infusion of technology has been a mixed blessing. Understand the necessary technologies that will make you more productive. Don't latch on to fads or gadgets that don't provide a productivity advantage.
- **Apply Lean Techniques.** Just as they were outlined in Chapter 5, the Lean Techniques will help you organize your workplace and home work areas to eliminate wasted motion and increase speed of completing tasks.

Managing Time

Effective time management goes beyond the basics of scheduling appointments and making daily to-do lists. Although these activities are important, the key to time management is to control your environment, not be controlled by it. We all have the same amount of time to use: 24 hours in a day, or 1,440 minutes. If this is true, why are some of us more productive in using this precious resource?

When you think of time management competency and what excellence looks like, would you say this is you?

- Considers time a valued resource.
- Concentrates efforts on the most urgent and important priorities.
- Focuses on how to get more done in less time.
- Doesn't waste energy and motion and has a clock in his/her head.

Time Wasters

A major reason that some managers are more productive than others is because the best managers are able to deal with time wasters and distractions that consume precious time and derail the most mission-critical work needed at any given point in time. The most common time wasters identified by managers were:

- **Crisis management:** constantly dealing with unplanned events that must get done.
- **Procrastination:** putting off completion of a task until a future date, possibly because you want to think more about it.
- **Ineffective meetings:** meetings that are poorly planned, waste time, and don't impact productivity.
- **Interruptions:** disruptions in your plans due to telephone calls and drop-in visitors.
- **Lack of plans and priorities:** each day starts out the same, working on priorities that seem most important without analyzing what's the best use of your time at that moment.

If any of these time wasters are particularly difficult for you or a staff member, take time to analyze the major causes for the time loss and develop a strategy to reduce or eliminate the time waster. Since procrastination appears on many lists as a top time waster, one way to address it is to develop a "do it now" attitude in which you will take some action on every priority. If you create some immediate momentum for action, you have a much better chance of finishing the rest of the task before you slip behind.

Planning for Results

The key to successful time management is to plan for results by working on those priorities that are both mission-critical and time-sensitive. These are the first priority actions. Action items that are mission-critical but not time-sensitive can be phased in with an action plan while working the first priority action items. Activities that are time-sensitive but not mission-critical should be

WORK HARDER

One of the myths of time management that has been debunked over the years is that you must work harder, work more hours, to be productive. Many professional "knowledge" workers spend countless hours on the job and may have the attitude that the number of hours spent on the job somehow equates to getting more accomplished. The reverse of that may actually be true. Setting priorities and managing time are the best measures of how to spend productive time.

evaluated. In most cases, these action items can be delegated. Those activities that aren't mission-critical or time-sensitive should be eliminated. These types of activities do end up on to-do lists, but should not remain there if they don't add value. Use the planning chart shown in Exhibit 10-1 to map out where your priorities fit. You can actually write them into the appropriate quadrants to determine the exact fit.

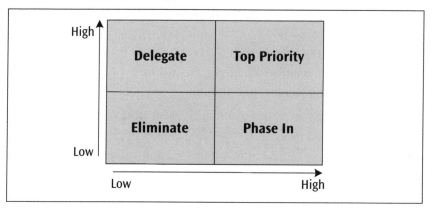

Exhibit 10-1. Figuring out your priorities

Managing Meetings

We've all heard the comments made after a poor meeting: "That was a complete waste of time," "Why was I asked to attend?" or "When will a meeting ever end on time?" With all that has been written about meeting effectiveness, abuse of time in meetings is still a large problem in organizations.

When you think of meeting management competency and what excellence looks like, would you say this is you?

- Plans meetings that consistently have objectives and agendas and lead to productive use of time spent in meetings. If action items are generated in a meeting, they are documented and reviewed for completion.
- Meetings lead to action.

Three Types of Meeting

A major problem with planning for a successful meeting is that a clear purpose may not have been identified prior to deciding the agenda and participation. The purpose of the meeting will determine how you'll arrive at your objective, how you'll lead the meeting, and who should attend. The problem that occurs is that meeting purposes are mixed together and that dilutes their focus and successful orchestration. There are three main types of meetings. By using the planning chart, you can lead your meeting for a successful outcome every time. It's helpful to define the type of meeting on the agenda so that participants will know how to prepare.

All About Meetings

SMART MANAGING

Informational Meetings

- **Purpose:** To present information in such a way that the meeting participants understand it and can use it.
- **Participation:** Any team member who has a need to use the information to perform their jobs.
- **Leadership:** Led by the person who has the most access to the information and can convey it to the participants.
- **Communication and Decision Making:** Usually one-way from the leader to participants. An opportunity to ask questions is useful. Decisions have already been made regarding the information presented.

Advisory Meetings

- **Purpose:** To obtain advice or information that the meeting leader needs to make a decision, solve a problem, or initiate a course of action.
- **Participation:** Those team members who are qualified to give input on the information required by the meeting leader.
- **Leadership:** Meeting should be led by a person who either needs the information directly or who is designated by a higher-level manager.
- **Communication and Decision Making:** Communication is primarily from team members to team leader. Any decisions regarding the information discussed should be communicated to the participants after the meeting has concluded.

Problem-Solving Meetings

- **Purpose:** To develop a working solution to a specific team problem.
- **Participation:** Team members who have the authority to make decisions regarding the solution to the problem or who are closest to the problem and can provide expert input. Normally, this input should be accomplished in an advisory meeting.

- **Leadership:** Led by the person who can most effectively lead the team and can make the final decision regarding a course of action.
- **Communication and Decision Making:** Communication is three-way, between meeting leader and participants and among participants. The team has the decision-making authority; if not this should be considered an advisory meeting.

TOO Method

The acronym TOO stands for Topic, Objectives, and Outline. One of the major shortcomings of impromptu meetings is that no agenda is available for the meeting. The meeting leader may articulate the purpose of the meeting and then move right into a discussion of the topic. These types of meetings often fall short of intended results and participants see much wasted time. One way to avoid this problem is to use the TOO protocol for each meeting. If an agenda cannot be prepared in advance, a TOO can be posted on a white board or flip chart at the onset of the meeting. Here is how it works:

Identify the Topic. A topic is the theme of the meeting. It's the anticipated focus on the meeting discussion and the "why" behind the participants' coming together. Themes can be drawn from issues or problems facing the department. It's also possible to brainstorm or provide a list of topics and have the participants prioritize in order of mission-critical and time-sensitive to determine what's the best use of their time during the meeting. Use the rule of only one topic or theme per meeting. The topic can be stated in terms of a question, such as "What is the most effective way to reduce transcription errors in the Medical Records Department?"

Establish the Objectives. The objectives are the expected outcomes and results of the meeting that the meeting leader and participants are jointly working toward. The objectives are based on the selected topic and should be attainable in the meeting format and time budgeted for the discussion. The objectives also serve as the evaluation criteria for meeting effectiveness.

Prepare the Outline. The outline contains the steps the meeting leader and participants will follow to attain the meeting objectives. These action steps are "how" the meeting will flow to get the expected results. The outline

The Parking Lot

During meeting discussions, questions and issues arise that may be beyond the scope of the meeting. If the meeting leader tries to address them, the meeting can easily go off track and fall short of achieving its objectives. A technique that helps to capture these questions and issues is the parking lot idea. When a question or issue comes up that's beyond the scope of the current meeting time and agenda, the meeting leader has the option of "parking" the question or issue on a flip chart.

This is called the parking lot and is a method of documenting and saving the question or issue for a wrap-up at the meeting conclusion. If this doesn't work, the meeting leader can follow up with participants by providing the answers in the meeting minutes.

should be framed in numerical steps, with estimated times for each step as a parameter to determine when to move on from a discussion.

Effective Presentations

When you think about the opportunities that you have to present information to one or more people, you may find that these opportunities are frequent and often informal. In fact, you could say that your day is composed of a series of presentations. The goal of an effective presenter is to treat every opportunity to interact with others as a forum to send clear messages, get your point across, and to listen for comments and feedback that may help you to further clarify your message.

Use the "elevator pitch" to spread the word about your business, communicate your departmental mission, strengthen professional and personal relationships, and increase your ability to influence others. In the time it takes you to ride an elevator with a stranger, you can present your capabilities and mission to anyone outside or inside the company.

To prepare a 30- to 60-second elevator speech about your department, think about a way to introduce yourself and the department in a memorable way. Use a tag line or emphasize the benefits or solutions your department provides to internal or external customers. Take the opportunity to highlight the department's uniqueness, special skills, and people. Show some excitement in explaining this information, especially to someone whom you don't know.

Survival Skills for Presenters

This short guide can help individuals who must deliver on-the-job presentations to overcome their fear of public speaking, understand the mechanics of presenting, and use group dynamics to their advantage. Since the main goal is to communicate effectively with your audience, these suggestions should serve as quick tips for success.

Analyze

- **Analyze Yourself**—Why will you be presenting? What's the purpose of your presentation? Why should your audience be interested in what you have to say?
- **Analyze Your Audience**—What's the background of your audience? What are their primary interests? What do they know about the topic of your presentation? What questions are they likely to ask about the topic?
- **Analyze Your Situation**—At what time of the day will you be presenting? How much material do you need to cover and in what period of time? How large is the group you'll be presenting to? What's the presentation venue (room size, etc.)?

Organize

Now that you've completed your analysis, begin to format your presentation into three components. The first component is the introduction. Use it to grab the attention of the audience, establish your credibility, and give a short overview of your objectives and what you'll cover. The second component is the body. Use it to craft your message into two or three main points that are logically sequenced so that the audience can easily follow it and can comprehend the information at a comfortable pace. The third component is the conclusion. It should be a short review of the key points covered in the body and should close with an attention grabber or call to action. Don't memorize your presentation or plan to read it to the audience.

Create Interest

Create interest in your presentation by using quotes, stories, analogies, humor, statistics, and audience participation. Each one of these options must be relevant to the topic and to the point. You can facilitate audience participation by asking open-ended questions. Be careful not to allow the participation to take too much time or take the presentation off track.

Practice

The idea behind practicing your presentation is to gain enough familiarity with the flow so that the words come out effortlessly and naturally. Through the practice you'll become more at ease, and be able to stay on track and finish in the allotted time.

Create Platform Presence

Create a presence before an audience through your appearance, language choices, pace, and volume. Be sure to vary your volume and articulate your words. Consciously avoid "um" and "ah" as you pause. Don't move around in front of the audience, as this will emphasize your nervousness. Use gestures occasionally to stimulate the audience and gain attention.

Use Media Effectively

Audiovisual materials can be a good complement to the spoken word. Be careful to make sure that slides meet legibility standards and that DVD and video playback can be seen and heard by the entire audience. All the equipment and information presented through the use of media should be tested in advance of the presentation and just before being used.

Perform a Lessons Learned Analysis

After each presentation, you should perform a Lessons Learned Analysis as described in Chapter 8. Feedback either

USE OF HUMOR

CAUTION

If you're planning to use humor in your presentation, it's important that you know your audience. This will give you a basis for selecting the type of humor that will work. The danger of using humor is that if it's poorly delivered or poorly received, your credibility will be lost with some or most of the audience. This will obviously have a negative impact on the overall presentation and your message may get lost because of it. It's best to bounce your plans to use humor off a trusted peer to test it first. This should give you an idea of how it may be received by your audience. One good source of humor is *Reader's Digest*. The humorous stories and anecdotes are straightforward and will work for most audiences. Make sure the humor fits your topic and keep it short.

in a written evaluation or verbally can help to identify strengths and weaknesses. This is especially helpful if you'll be repeating the presentation or transferring the learning to your next presentation.

Negotiations

Negotiation is a discussion intended to resolve disputes, to produce an agreement direction and action steps, to bargain, or to satisfy various interests. The styles used in a negotiation will often determine the outcome of the discussion, either positive or negative. Stalemates are also a common outcome of style differences or clashes. Think about your own style and think about which styles most represent the way you negotiate.

The competitive style is focused on winning at all costs. This style exhibits a high degree of assertiveness, but it does not encourage cooperation from the other party. Opposite to this is the avoidance style, which is focused on avoiding conflict and any real engagement in a meaningful discussion. The accommodating style focuses on pleasing the other party and may easily slide into a competitive style.

Sometimes in customer-related situations, a customer service person may make every attempt to accommodate the requests of a highly competitive customer who won't give up until their position is satisfied. The compromising style focuses on making a deal. On the surface this seems like an effective style. In reality, striking a deal may create a winner and loser, intentionally or unintentionally. The collaborative style is the most effective and focuses on learning the interests of the other party and trying to achieve mutually agreed-upon outcomes or solutions.

The most effective solutions include the interests of both parties in some way. This style may be more difficult to achieve or more time-consuming to attain, but it does create the most sustaining agreements. You may want to review the Harvard Business publication *Getting to Yes* to learn more about becoming a more effective negotiator and developing the ability to create more win-win outcomes.

Managing Relationships

During the planning and execution of business plans, there is a need to manage relationships with co-workers, your immediate manager, your direct reports (if applicable), and customers. The diagram in Exhibit 10-2 indicates that those relationships must be balanced and the best way to do this is to identify your objectives for each group.

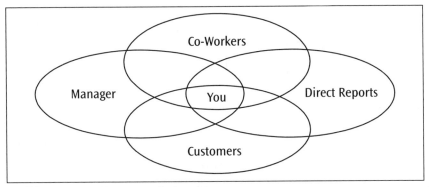

Exhibit 10-2. Overlapping relationships

For example, your objectives for your manager would include a clear understanding of your performance standards, agreement on a coaching process, and amount of flexibility you have in decision making. For your customers, your objectives would include a clear understanding of their requirements and a periodic assessment of how well you are meeting those requirements. These objectives can become part of your formal performance standards or monitored informally every two to three months.

Making a Commitment to Change for the Better

To develop competencies in the skill areas of planning and execution, it's critical to commit to begin new techniques, leverage your current strengths, and break old habits that don't contribute to achieving excellence. From the learning you've gained from reading this book, identify at least one action for the following questions, asking "What will I continue doing, start doing, and stop doing to be a more successful planner and executor of plans?" Write down one bullet point for each one and make a conscious effort to focus on making a change.

Your Continuing Development Plan

Consideration for creating your development plan requires a structured approach to defining your goals and then creating a supporting plan to achieve them. One manager learned that there was a lack of customer satisfaction data for the purpose of creating baseline data and planning for improvements to support the company goal of increased customer retention. The sample plan he used is included here. It should serve as a model to prepare your personal development plan for self-directed learning and continuous improvement.

Just-in-time learning is a way to request coaching or mentoring from your immediate manager or a respected peer on selected opportunities. This can occur during your day-to-day interactions while working on a particular skill or behavior adjustment.

It's also a good idea to practice the skill and model your style from other managers who are good at the skill. Seeking feedback from a trusted peer, mentor (peer coaching), or immediate manager will help you identify and reinforce your progress.

Invest in learning by taking courses, obtaining certifications, using the Internet, reading, and using audiotapes. You can structure your approach using this sample development plan.

SAMPLE TEMPLATE: INDIVIDUAL DEVELOPMENT PLAN

TOOLS

Name: _____ Date: _____

Position: _____ Department: _____

Immediate Manager: _____

A. Development Areas: Identify the overall improvement needs.
- Develop a process to monitor customer satisfaction.

B. Development Goals: Define the goals. Make them specific and measurable (one goal for each development area).
- Learn techniques for how to gather and measure customer satisfaction and apply them in my department in the second quarter.

C. Action Plan/Steps: List the specific actions you will take to improve.
- Research best practices in monitoring customer satisfaction.

- Search the Internet and bookstores to identify resources.
- Speak with the internal quality department to identify available tools.
- Select a tool/survey and conduct a pilot with my internal customers by _____.
- Review the feedback, share with the department, and make improvements as required.
- Standardize the process for an annual frequency.

D. **Involvement of Others:** Identify individuals who can help.
- Immediate manager (for support), department team members, external/internal customers.

E. **Target Dates:** List the timeframe for completion of the action plan. Use item C above as a reference.
- Conduct research by _____.
- Have a discussion with the quality manager regarding use of tools by _____.
- Select a tool to use for a pilot survey by _____.
- Send the survey to a group of key internal customers by _____.
- Review the feedback, evaluate the process, and begin improvements by _____.
- Standardize the process for fiscal year (FY) _____.

Balancing Work and Personal Life

Striking a balance between your work priorities and personal priorities so that neither is neglected can be an enormous challenge. There is no single method or process that works for everyone. The priorities of work and personal life can be dictated by our personal style preferences, so learning about oneself can help make adjustments when there's a lack of desired balance. Here are some suggestions to think about:

1. Do an assessment of where you are currently setting your priorities and determine if the balance is correct for you. Look for warning signs that an imbalance exists, like missing key family events or not being available at times when you're needed.

2. Establish guard rails and boundaries that set goals and targets to free up time to create a better balance in your work and personal life.

3. Create a network of people whom you trust to serve as mentors and shepherds. In these roles, they can give you feedback and guidance to help create the balance you desire.

4. Create a more flexible work schedule. If you need more personal time, create this time at the beginning or end of the day. If you need time in the morning to devote to family, consider staying later at work, and vice versa if late afternoons are more important for family time.

5. Integrate work and family whenever possible. Sometimes work events like preparing for meetings, team luncheons, and social hours allow for spouse involvement. Company-sponsored events like picnics and charity events can also be good times to integrate your family.

Manager's Checklist for Chapter 10

☑ Use the best practice information to improve your organizational and time management skills.

☑ Apply the survival guide for presenters on your next presentation.

☑ Improve the quality and productivity of your meetings using the Topic, Objective, Outline format.

☑ Use your ability to strategize relationships and negotiate to guide the planning and execution process.

☑ Complete a personal development plan to continue your focus on learning.

Appendix

Planning Toolkit

Planning Toolkit

O ne of the most critical aspects of orchestrating a planning process is the engagement of others to support the collection and analysis of data to help you turn it into useful information. This appendix provides you with a set of tools that will help you do this so you can create plans that lead to successful actions. The days of a few managers having all the responsibility for the business plan, from inception to completion, are all but gone. There are distinct advantages to involving others in planning, analysis, and problem solving, including buy-in and ownership of the planned results.

This toolkit may be utilized in several situations described in this book including:

- Analysis of data for the plan.
- Creating baseline measurement and tracking objectives.
- Deployment and mobilizing of the workforce.

You'll find specific applications of planning and problem-solving techniques explained in detail, using a fictitious company called Aztec Manufacturing to demonstrate the use and application of these tools.

Applying Planning and Problem-Solving Tools

The ability to identify and act on opportunities and issues that impact business performance is the key to success in today's marketplace. The amount of unplanned and unforeseen change continues to increase. The application of these tools will help to eliminate crisis management or reactive behavior if they are used in the manner suggested in this appendix.

Seven Tools Everyone Should Know

A major gap exists in the employee-empowered workplace emphasized by many companies today. On the one hand, employees are expected to know more and do more, on the other hand they receive limited training on how to plan and solve problems. Mastering seven tools is critical for success in the corrective action process with a team or individual. The tools are *brainstorming, flowcharting, check sheets, Pareto diagram, cause-and-effect (fishbone) diagrams, prioritization matrices,* and *action plan guidelines.* Although all these tools will be covered in detail, a quick Internet search will provide additional information on how to execute them successfully.

Toolkit Planning Chart

The *toolkit planning chart,* shown in Exhibit 1, is designed to provide a quick reference guide to enhance the planning and problem-solving processes. You can scan the matrix to determine the need and appropriate tools that will help to facilitate the identification of opportunities and a plan to take action on them. It can also help to engage and focus people during the process.

Tools \ When to Use	Get People Focused	Identify Opportunties and Issues	Understand the Situation	Rank or Prioritize Decisions	Develop Actions
Brainstorming	✔	✔		✔	✔
Flowchart		✔	✔		
Cause-and-Effect Diagram		✔	✔		
Check sheet		✔	✔		
Pareto Diagram	✔	✔			
Prioritization Matrix				✔	
Action Plan	✔				✔

Exhibit 1. Planning tools and when to use them

Getting People Involved

There are two parts to successfully involving people in the planning process. First is obviously getting the right people into the process at the right time to tap into their experience, ideas, and ability to be valued resources. The second part is to facilitate their participation in a positive and productive manner. The tools available here will help to guide that participation in every aspect of identifying and addressing issues uncovered in the planning process.

Brainstorming

Brainstorming is a versatile tool that uses group creativity to generate a large volume of ideas that people can later refine. Its power is based on both the spontaneity of free association and the encouragement of full participation within a "safe" environment.

When used. Brainstorming has a multitude of applications. It is used to identify possible issues, opportunities, root causes, and solutions. It is important to use brainstorming in tandem with other tools.

TIPS FOR BRAINSTORMING

To effectively guide a brainstorming session, use the following quick tips to get a positive result:

- Offer one idea at a time.
- Avoid paraphrasing or changing ideas.
- Don't evaluate the ideas. The goal is to get as many ideas as possible.
- Avoid criticism or praise of ideas.
- Strive for full participation.
- Build on the ideas of others.
- Don't quit too soon. Many good ideas can be generated after a lull.

Aztec Manufacturing experienced an unusually high number of customer complaints regarding their shipping process. Since customer satisfaction was a key objective for the company, they began to immediately address the improvement opportunity.

As a result of a brainstorming session the following issues were indentified for further investigation: damaged cartons, wrong quantities, wrong items, and late shipments.

Identifying Issues and Challenges

Being able to get at the issues will be a great help when tracking and influencing outcomes. Use of these tools will help to avoid the tendency to reach premature conclusions. One of the best tools to apply to process and work flow situations is the flowchart. This tool should be combined with brainstorming to help engage people in the exercise.

Flowcharting

Flowcharts are used to clearly describe in pictorial form the sequence of steps in a process and the relationships between them.

When used. Use flowcharts in existing or ideal situations to document, analyze, or develop a path of activities or steps in a process, Flowcharts are used in process improvement to uncover loopholes, delays, and non-value-added activities. Exhibit 2 shows the typical symbols used in creating a flowchart.

Aztec Manufacturing decided to evaluate its order fulfillment process to determine if there were any improvements that could be made to streamline the process, as shown in Exhibit 3.

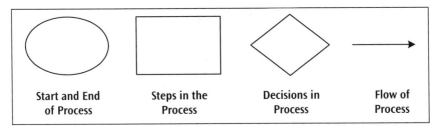

Exhibit 2. Basic symbols used in flowcharting

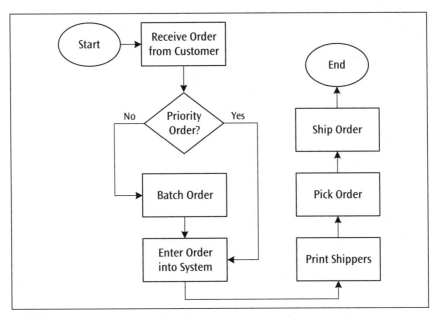

Exhibit 3. An example of a flowchart for Aztec's order processing

Flowcharting Tips

- Determine the appropriate starting and ending boundaries of the process.
- Don't flowchart a large process. Break it down into sub-processes.
- Ask, "What happens next?"
- Keep the flowchart clear and simple.
- Show all decision steps, feedback loops, and wait loops.
- Look for ways to simplify, shorten, and improve the process being flowcharted.

Identifying Opportunities and Issues

The focus of every organization should be on continuous improvement. The first priority is to deal with issues that arise during execution of plans, especially when objectives are falling short of expectations. Using the review processes discussed in Chapter 3 for measuring performance and the contingency planning techniques discussed in Chapter 7, you will be alerted to issues and opportunities. Acting quickly using the tools and techniques available will ensure positive results. Both check sheets and Pareto diagrams will be important aids to pinpointing the right issues and opportunities.

Check sheets

Check sheets are used to gather data that quantify how often, where, and when certain events occur (usually undesirable events such as errors, defects, variations, or process failures). Check sheets translate "opinions" about a problem or situation into "facts."

When used. Check sheets are used to help collect improvement opportunities, verify root causes, and measure the effectiveness of improvements.

1. Agree on what the check sheet will capture. What events will you look for? Be specific so everyone looks for the same things.
2. Determine the time period in which data will be collected. When will the collection period begin and end? Will they be used hourly, daily, weekly, monthly, or on an ongoing basis?
3. Create the check sheet. Is it easy to understand and use? Does it capture all the required data?
4. Collect the data. Be consistent and unbiased. Allow adequate time for accurate data collection. Be sure statistically valid samples are used. Let the data speak for themselves. Analyzing the data will be

easier and more revealing if the check sheets are well designed and carefully used.

As a first step to determine the most important improvement opportunity regarding shipping problems, Aztec Manufacturing used a check sheet, shown in Exhibit 4, to identify the areas to focus on.

Pareto Chart

Check sheet					
Shipping Problems			Month _____		
	Week 1	Week 2	Week 3	Week 4	TOTAL
Damaged Cartons	/		//	/	4
Late Shipments	//	-/////	-///// ///	-///// -///// //	27
Wrong Quantity	///	/	//	//	8
Wrong Item Shipped		/	//	///	6
TOTAL	6	7	14	18	45

Exhibit 4. A check sheet for tracking Aztec shipping problems

A Pareto chart is a special type of vertical bar chart that visually compares numerical data, usually from check sheet information. It displays from greatest to least the frequency of occurrences such as types of problems, costs of problems, problems by product, or various other measurements. This visual aid will help identify the most significant issues that need to be corrected.

When used. Pareto charts are used to choose the most significant problem to solve. They can also be used to track the effectiveness of improvement efforts and measure the impact of solutions.

After using the check sheet, Aztec Manufacturing then decided to further verify the late shipments as a focus area by using a Pareto chart, as shown in Exhibit 5.

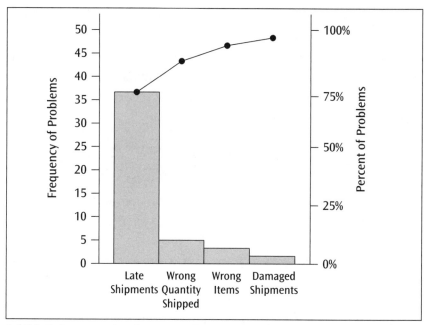

Exhibit 5. An example of a Pareto chart, which shows where Aztec needs to focus its energy to solve shipping problems

Based on this Pareto chart, by reducing late shipments they can reduce the majority of shipping problems. This is an example of the "80/20 rule of thumb" (roughly 80% of an overall effect can often be traced back to about 20% of all contributing causes of influences).

Understanding the Situation

To understand a situation, you must have clarity regarding what is happening and identify the measurable magnitude of the opportunity or issue. This should include information such as frequency, cost, delays, trends, etc. One of the best tools to accomplish this task is the cause-and-effect diagram.

Cause-and-Effect (Fishbone) Diagram

The cause-and-effect diagram (also called a fishbone diagram because of the way it looks) is used to represent the relationship between the effect of a problem or situation and all the possible causes of that effect. The cause-and-effect diagram can be more effectively created when populated with the information gained from brainstorming, check sheets, and Pareto diagrams.

When used. The cause-and-effect diagram can be used to sort out and identify possible root causes of a problem. It can also be used to identify causes of a desirable effect, a variation called "reverse cause and effect." This is useful to understand the positive impacts of a situation and what works well.

1. Create an effect statement. Write it in a box at the far right of a flip chart.
2. Choose categories of possible causes. Potential categories: materials, methods, machines, environment, procedures, technology, or human factors. Use four to five major categories that help people think creatively.
3. Construct the diagram and brainstorm causes. Draw the skeleton of the diagram and label each major branch with a category. Following the rules of brainstorming, ask "Under this category, what is causing (the effect) to happen?" Be specific. Post all ideas that branch off the appropriate category.
4. Brainstorm "causes of the causes." After brainstorming causes, go to the next level by asking, "What causes this cause?" Post these ideas as branches off of the original cause. A third or fourth level may be necessary. Keep digging!
5. Analyze the completed diagram. Look for causes that appear repeatedly, for causes that the team feels are most significant, and for causes that are likely candidates for further analysis using data collection and fact-gathering.

Example of a Cause-and-Effect Diagram

The small manufacturing company determined that the cause of late shipments was its focus area and decided to use a cause-and-effect diagram to identify specific causes and contributors to the late shipment issue. This tool (Exhibit 6) will help to identify causes, effects, and improvement opportunities that will provide the information required to keep the business plan objectives on track.

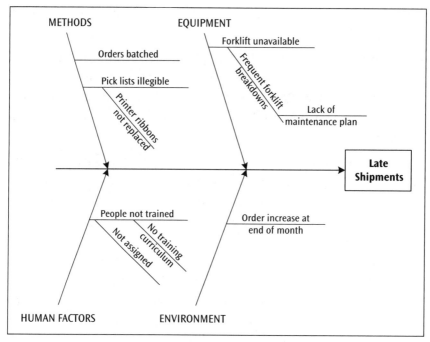

Exhibit 6. A cause-and-effect diagram for identifying the causes of late shipments

Ranking or Prioritizing for Decisions

This tool is designed to support decision making, which will then lead into the action plan.

Use of the prioritization matrix will create a confidence factor in the accuracy of the decision and increase the speed of decisions.

Prioritization Matrix

The prioritization matrix is used because it's an effective tool for analysis and decision making. It helps prioritize actions so resources can be assigned and action plans can be developed.

In this example, assume that there are five team members participating in the exercise. The results are displayed in Exhibit 7.

1. Develop a list of criteria to apply to the options. Use wording that reflects a desired outcome, e.g., low cost to implement, quick to implement, easily accepted.

2. Create a matrix. List the options vertically and the criteria horizontally.

3. Rank the criteria. Each one of five members rank orders the criteria by distributing the total value of 1.0 among them (e.g., a member might give the criterion "low cost to implement" a .3 and "quick to implement" a lesser value of .2, while "easily accepted by users" receives a .5). Add up the ranking values of all members to compute a composite criterion ranking score (e.g., if five team members rank "low cost to implement" with a .2, .3, .2, .4, and .3, then its composite criterion score is 1.4). Place this composite criterion score in the appropriate cells of the matrix.

4. Rank the options. Each group member rank orders the options according to how well they meet each criterion, from most to least preferred. Add everyone's rankings together (e.g., if "low cost to implement" is ranked 2, 2, 3, 2, and 1 by the five team members, its composite score is 10). Reorder the list of options based on their composite scores, from high to low. Give the highest-numbered option a value of one, the next highest a value of two, etc., until all options are ranked per each criterion. Place each option's ranking number in the appropriate cell.

5. Compute the individual importance score for each option under each criterion. Multiply the composite criterion ranking score by the option ranking (e.g., a composite criterion score of 1.4 times an option ranking of 3 = 4.2).

6. Compute the total ranking scores across all criteria. Once individual scores have been calculated for all options under each criterion, add scores together across all the criteria. The option with the highest number becomes the highest priority and the remaining options can be ranked in order of decreasing priority.

Criteria / Option	Low Cost to Implement 1.4	Quick to Implement 2.3	Easily Accepted .8	TOTAL
Option A	1 x 1.4 = 1.4	3 x 2.3 = 6.9	2 x .8 = 1.6	9.9
Option B	3 x 1.4 = 4.2	1 x 2.3 = 1.3	1 x .8 = .8	7.3
Option C	2 x 1.4 = 2.8	2 x 2.3 = 4.6	3 x .8 = 2.4	9.8

Exhibit 7. A prioritization matrix to help Aztec decide on which of three options to implement to solve a problem

Developing Actions

Taking actions regarding the data that has been gathered, analyzed, prioritized, and decided upon will ensure successful achievement of the performance objectives established in functional and individual plans.

Action Plan

Action plans are used because they promote thorough and measurable implementation of plans. With a solid Action Plan all members of a team know exactly what needs to be done, by whom, and when.

When used. Action plans are used for implementation of decisions made through the use of the tools illustrated here. They are used following a prioritization matrix to identify high-priority actions that need to be implemented to deploy a strategy. Critical projects and complex implementations may need advanced tools such as Critical Path planning, Project Evaluation and Review Technique (PERT), Gantt charts, Process Decision Program Charts (PDPC), or computerized project management tools. These tools can be found through an Internet search and literature review to identify additional sources of information.

Action Plan Tips.
- Good action plans are time-based.
- Good action plans have goal statements.
- Get consensus from all involved groups.
- Develop measurements to track the plan.
- Use PDCA (Plan, Do, Check, Act) to check and improve the plan.

- Allow flexibility in how actions are to be accomplished.
- Maintain accountability.

Aztec Manufacturing decided that as a result of their analyses, forklift maintenance would require immediate attention and developed the following action plan to make the improvement.

Goal: Reduce shipping delays caused by lack of forklift maintenance from 22 delays per month to 5 delays per month by year end.

What	Measurement	Who	When	Status
Create library of forklift maintenance manuals	100% of manuals available	Jim Kelly	June 1	Complete
Develop and implement maintenance training program	Course presented	Training Dept.	June 22	70% Complete
Create maintenance plan	Maintenance plan implemented	Raymond	July 22	Complete
Implement certification program for forklift drivers	100% of drivers certified	Training Dept.	Sept. 30	Need to identify trainers

Exhibit 8. Sample action plan for Aztec Manufacturing

Manager's Checklist for the Planning Toolkit

☑ Utilize the toolkit planning chart to identify the tools that may be appropriate to your need.

☑ Select the tools and techniques that will assist in creating, tracking, and influencing measurements.

☑ Begin to use the planning and problem-solving tools in day-to-day planning and review situations.

☑ Utilize the cause-and-effect diagram and prioritization matrix to aid current understanding and decision making.

☑ Utilize the action plans as a benchmark against current practices.

Index

About the Author

Peter J. Capezio is the Principal of Value Added Resources and brings over 25 years of experience in Fortune 500 companies to the consulting arena. He has been involved in leading organization change and helping companies adapt to dynamic market conditions and improve overall results. The major emphasis of this work has been on developing and integrating business strategy and plans with organization planning and development. A key component of this work has been on deployment of plans for execution and implementation. Peter has held key managerial positions with Black and Decker, Becton Dickinson, Blue Cross & Blue Shield of Florida, St. Elizabeth's Hospital of Boston, and Wang Laboratories. He has demonstrated expertise in business and organization development, executive leadership, total quality initiatives, and building high-performing teams.

He started his consulting practice in 1991 and became a full-time consultant in 1997. Peter has been responsible for designing and implementing strategy and business plans focusing on operational excellence, leadership, and people development. He uses data collection and analysis via online surveys to define strengths and improvement opportunities. Peter received his bachelor's degree from Montclair State University (NJ) and a master's degree from Boston University. His formal education has focused primarily on business, industrial education, and learning systems. Peter has authored other books on the subjects of total quality management, team development, and leadership. Visit his website at www.valueaddedresources.net.

2010
—
2021
—
13